TIMES AND SEASONS:

A JEWISH PERSPECTIVE
FOR INTERMARRIED COUPLES

A GUIDE FOR FACILITATORS

Prepared by the
Commission on Reform Jewish Outreach
of the Union of American Hebrew Congregations
and the Central Conference of American Rabbis

Fall 1987

Table of Contents

Acknowledgements

UAHC-CCAR Commission on Reform Jewish Outreach

David Belin, Chairperson
Rabbi Steven Foster, Co-Chairperson
Lydia Kukoff, Director and
                Executive Editor, Times and Seasons...
                                  A Guide for Facilitators
Rabbi Nina J. Mizrahi, Assistant Director and
                Editor, Times and Seasons...
                                  A Guide for Facilitators

Regional Outreach Staff

Great Lakes Council/Chicago Federation: Mimi Dunitz
Mid-Atlantic Council: Elizabeth Farquhar
Midwest Council: Nancy Gad-Harf
New Jersey/West Hudson Valley Council: Dru Greenwood
New York Federation of Reform Synagogues: Dr. Carolyn Kunin
Northeast Council: Nancy Kelly Kleiman
Northeast Lakes Council/Detroit Federation:
                                           Rosette Barron Haim
Northern California Council: Miriam Rosenthal
Pacific Southwest Council: Arlene Chernow
Pennsylvania Council/Philadelphia Federation:
                                           Sherri Alper
                                           Rabbi Randi Musnitsky
Southeast Council/South Florida Federation:Rabbi Rachel Hertzman

Administrative Staff: Muriel Finn, Lillian Shapiro

Art Department: Rayleen Buys, Helayne Friedland

Copy Editor: Joy Weinberg

Editorial Committee: Sherri Alper, Dru Greenwood, David
                      Kasakove, Nancy Kelly Kleiman, Lydia
                      Kukoff, Rabbi Nina Mizrahi, Rabbi Joel
                      Oseran, Deborah Reshotko

****

We express our special gratitude to Rabbi Joel Oseran, co-developer of the "Times and Seasons..." program, for his many contributions to the manual and to the success of this program.

We thank the Pacific Southwest Council of the UAHC for serving as the testing site for "Times and Seasons...", Rabbi Lennard Thal, Director of the Pacific Southwest Council, for his valuable assistance at the inception of the program and Rabbi Daniel Bridge, Assistant Director. Additional thanks are expressed to Judith Aronson, R.J.E., a co-developer of the program and to the National Federation of Temple Sisterhoods, who helped to subsidize the pilot program.

And finally, we thank all facilitators, past, present and future, for reaching out and all couples who have participated in this program and who have taught us so much.

<u>Times and Seasons</u>

Part I: Background

The Reform Movement's Outreach Program

Objectives

What We Hope to Accomplish

Group Statistics

The Group and the Setting

The Facilitator

Targeting the Issues

Times and Seasons

The Reform Movement's Outreach Program

On December 2, 1978, Rabbi Alexander Schindler, President of the Union of American Hebrew Congregations (the congregational arm of the Reform Movement), called upon the Board of Trustees to establish a program of Outreach which would develop responses to the needs of individuals converting to Judaism, intermarried couples, children of intermarriages, and those interested in learning about Judaism. The UAHC Trustees unanimously adopted a resolution calling for the study and development of a program of Reform Jewish Outreach and endorsed the creation of a Joint Task Force with the Central Conference of American Rabbis. David Belin was named Chairman and Rabbi Max Shapiro as Co-Chair, who was followed by Rabbi Sheldon Zimmerman. This task force presented a report to the 1981 UAHC General Assembly, which then adopted five resolutions calling for a comprehensive program of Reform Jewish Outreach. (see appendix 3)

Since that time, the program has expanded and currently reaches out to:

* intermarried couples and couples contemplating intermarriage
* children of intermarried couples
* Jews-by-Choice and those in the process of choosing Judaism
* parents of intermarried couples

In 1983, the task force became a Joint UAHC-CCAR Commission on Reform Jewish Outreach with a mandate to develop programming, resources, and materials for Outreach target populations. Lydia Kukoff was named Commission Director, David Belin continued as Chairperson, and Rabbi Steven Foster became Co-Chair.

The Outreach staff has expanded and currently includes an Assistant Director, Rabbi Nina Mizrahi, and Outreach Coordinators in virtually every UAHC region. Coordinators serve as resources for each congregation in their region, working closely with the temple's professional staff and Outreach committee to design a suitable Outreach program for the congregation. Together, the regional coordinator, the temple's professional staff, and the Outreach committee integrate new Jews-by-Choice into the community. They welcome intermarried couples and their children, and educate and sensitize synagogue members about intermarriage and conversion in order to create a receptive climate in the congregation.

Also in 1983, the "Times and Seasons" program was created in response to the needs of the intermarried, to serve as the critical first step taken by unaffiliated intermarried couples seeking to explore differences in their backgrounds. Now it has become an important part of the Reform Movement's Outreach program throughout the United States. The UAHC trains new facilitators every year.

The facilitator's guide marks another step in the growth of this innovative program.

Objectives

The objectives of the program are:

1. To promote open communication between partners in order to strengthen their relationship.

2. To provide an opportunity for each member of the couple to explore the impact of religious tradition on his/her life.

3. To create a forum in which couples can learn and benefit from the experience and advice of others.

4. To clarify the major teachings of Judaism and the implications of establishing a Jewish home so that both the Jewish and non-Jewish partners can understand their connection to Judaism.

5. To communicate that the Reform Jewish community welcomes the intermarried couple and that the couple can find a place in the community.

The decision to establish a Jewish home and raise children as Jews is not a stated objective of the program, but rather an outcome we hope to accomplish.

What We Hope to Accomplish

Intermarriage (marriage between a Jew and a non-Jew) is significantly increasing, with clear potential to erode the future of Jewish life in America. In response, the Reform Movement is addressing the needs of hundreds of thousands of intermarried couples by encouraging them to become affiliated. The "Times and Seasons" program is based on the principle that there is a place for the intermarried couple and family within the organized Jewish community.

The group experience is designed to clarify the Jewish partner's feelings about Judaism and to provide the non-Jewish partner with a broader understanding of Judaism and the Jewish community. Relevant personal issues discussed include: family life as a child, religious involvement while growing up, meeting and falling in love with the partner, the religious and cultural issues each partner confronts in the relationship, and each couple's concerns about the religious identity of their children. Our position is that it is desirable for the couple to raise their children in one religious tradition. We hope that, as couples understand the benefits of rearing their children with a singular religious identity, they will ultimately choose Judaism for their children.

Although the program presents the Jewish perspective, there is no attempt to convert the non-Jewish partner. Judaism is not presented as the better religious tradition and non-Jewish partners are not asked to abandon their religious identification.

Many participants are not ready or willing to evaluate their connection to their religious tradition; yet this is critical to the discussion process. Before participants discuss religious options for their children, they must clarify the religious identity they wish to transmit. Group discussion concerning childrearing is designed not to take place until participants have gained a solid understanding of Judaism and its meaning in their lives. First, the intermarried couple will learn how a Jewish home reflects Jewish religious, cultural, and educational values, traditions, and observances; then the couple will explore their own goals regarding home and family life.

Partners often enter the group believing it is good to minimize the differences between their religious traditions; the program, however, stresses the significant differences between Judaism and Christianity. We believe that understanding these differences will allow fuller communication between partners.

Times and Seasons

Group Statistics

"Times and Seasons" is open to intermarried couples and couples contemplating intermarriage. Although each group of 5-8 couples is different, we can make a number of generalizations.

Couples range in age from mid-20's through mid-40's; about 75% are unmarried; often there is a majority of Jewish men in the group. Some married couples may have very young children, or, occasionally, children from a previous marriage, but most couples are childless. Generally, participants are highly educated, with at least a B.A. degree, and work full-time in white-collar professions.

Most participants show great respect for their partners' religious background and traditions. Almost all couples without children are content with their status quo arrangement for holiday celebrations and other religious and cultural observances. The most common factor influencing couples to attend the group is the desire to discuss childrearing in an intermarried family.

Couples enter the program at different stages of an intermarried relationship. Couples who have been together for many years share accumulated experiences which give their relationship rich history. Couples with children have been forced to confront certain practical questions relating to life cycle events. Unmarried couples may have very different experiences. Couples also differ in their openness and ease in confronting issues in their relationship.

Participation in the program seems to cause greater stress for couples who have not made a formal commitment than for those engaged or married. An unmarried couple may use the group experience as a test of marital compatibility, whereas a married couple usually understands that the issues must be resolved by a mutually satisfying compromise.

Times and Seasons

Experience has shown that the program may not be appropriate for couples who have already decided to establish a Jewish home and raise their children as Jews. In such cases, the couple can be referred to a different program, such as an Introduction to Judaism class, which provides a more in-depth study of Judaism.

Times and Seasons

The Group and the Setting

The ideal number of couples in a group is seven, with a minimum of five and a maximum of eight.

Groups usually meet for two hours, starting at 7:30 pm. Couples should understand that regular attendance is vital for developing rapport within the group and understanding the issues. Even if one partner of a couple cannot attend a session, the other should come. If neither member can attend, the couple should call the group facilitator. New couples should not be added after the first week.

The preferred setting for the group is a synagogue. The temple serves as a concrete expression of the Jewish community's willingness to welcome the couples, a critical message of the "Times and Seasons" program. If a temple is not available, the group can meet in a Jewish communal agency.

Within the temple, we recommend using the synagogue library for the sessions, so that participants have the opportunity to browse among the books. (Make arrangements to enable participants to check out books if they wish.) The sanctuary or the chapel should not be used. The room should contain comfortable chairs arranged in a circle, a blackboard, and a table for refreshments.

After a few meetings, you may wish to give participants a tour of the building, to help them feel at home in the synagogue.

Times and Seasons

The Facilitator

The role of facilitator will be challenging and demanding. To a great extent, your effectiveness depends upon being prepared. Preparedness requires anticipating issues likely to be raised and considering how to respond sensitively and honestly. Preparedness also implies being aware of your feelings, opinions, and vulnerabilities. Understand that group members are searching for their religious identity and often have more questions than answers. They will look to you for solutions, while at the same time expressing skepticism toward any answer which compromises the happiness of either partner.

How can you prepare yourself to be a facilitator? Search your innermost thoughts and feelings concerning intermarriage, Jewish survival, and rabbinic officiation at intermarriages. Discover your biases, fears, and convictions before entering the group. Understand that the discussions will trigger many deep feelings.

<u>You are a facilitator promoting honest dialogue betwen group members</u>. While it may be tempting to act as a therapist, psychologist, or marriage and family counselor, remember that your role is to help the group clarify questions and issues, not to analyze problems in search of an ultimate solution.

<u>You are a committed Jew and an excellent teacher of Judaism</u>, sufficiently knowledgeable to answer participants' questions about Jewish traditions, teachings, and observances. You should teach by making brief comments about Jewish practice whenever possible in order to provide insights and background information. You may wish to add brief anecdotes about your own experiences.

<u>You are the architect of the group experience</u>.

Create a sense of trust and support in the group, so that participants will feel free to articulate sensitive issues.

Times and Seasons

Find the delicate balance between being the advocate for Judaism and being accepting of individual behavior which contradicts your beliefs. Never take an adversarial position which would lead to a "you vs. them" situation; you are not the embodiment of the Jewish establishment whose task it is to show the group the error of its ways. The group should feel that you understand their position even if you do not agree with their actions.

Allow participants to express themselves fully. Otherwise, they will sense that certain points of view are out of bounds and will stop voicing their feelings. Let group members voice contrary opinions whenever possible, and seek out positions on sensitive issues before explaining your own. If a group member articulates a position against dual rearing of children, for example, it will carry more weight than your saying the same thing.

Express your own feelings as one party in a group dialogue, not as a censor or authoritarian group leader, and do not respond to every statement. Although you may be tempted to correct inaccurate statements or react to provocative comments, you must prevent the discussion from becoming a dialogue between individual members and yourself.

Anticipate that the group may try to manipulate you into agreeing with their position, assuming that if you support the intermarried couples in the group, then you support intermarriage. In subtle ways, the group may influence you to sanction dual rearing of children, dual celebration of Chanukah and Christmas in the home, etc. As facilitator, you should not validate these positions.

Maintain a sense of humor, which will prevent "heaviness" during sensitive discussions, keep perspective, and add to the enjoyment of the group.

You are sensitive to group dynamics.

Sometimes group members are reticent because they are unsure of themselves and/or their position. Encourage a particularly shy individual to participate by asking direct questions or phoning during the week to offer support. Conversely, you should prevent any individual from dominating the discussion. Regardless of the group dynamics at a given moment, the group should feel at all times that it is subject to your leadership and direction.

Occasionally couples are threatened by the discussion early on in the group and conclude that it is better to avoid the issues. If a couple fails to attend a session, contact them to find out why. If they have decided not to continue in the group, explore the reasons for the decision and offer appropriate counsel. Keep in mind that the program is not appropriate for every couple; partners should not continue if tensions are running explosively high.

Couples may be at different stages of an intermarried relationship. Some partners may talk about everything, whereas others may not discuss the most obvious problems. Never assume that partners have previously discussed the crucial issues relating to intermarriage. Look closely at individual couples to understand their specific needs.

The group experience may have significant impact upon the Jewish partners' understanding of and relationship to Judaism. Some may be relieved to have help in articulating the meaning of Judaism in their lives. Others may be anxious and even hostile about the program's position of raising children as Jews, perceiving the program as an attempt to convert their partner. Be cautious and sensitive to these reactions, and defuse such concerns immediately.

Often the Jewish partner feels uncomfortable about not knowing how to be Jewish. Reassure him/her about the numerous ways to acquire a fuller knowledge of Judaism. If couples choose to maintain a Jewish home, the Jewish partner should and will be able to bear the major responsibility for establishing it. Opportunities for continued Jewish study and involvement will be discussed during the program.

The reactions of the non-Jewish partners will vary. Some use the program as a tentative first step to learning more about Judaism and Jews. Others may feel threatened, at least initially, by the Jewish perspective of the program, and fear that

their feelings as non-Jews will be perceived as less valid. Alleviate these fears at the
beginning of the program by reminding all participants to feel free to express their views.
Experience shows that even those non-Jewish partners who feel uncomfortable at the
beginning of the program become at ease once they realize that their presence and insights
are valued.

Targeting the Issues

"Times and Seasons" is designed to discuss aspects of Judaism which distinguish Judaism from Christianity. (see appendix 1) In a supportive, constructive way, participants learn that, while they as a couple may choose to minimize basic historical, idelogical, or theological differences between religions, the outside world often reinforces them. Discussion on the differences between Judaism and Christianity is not intended to imply that Judaism is the better religion or that the non-Jew should convert to Judaism.

Religious Identity

To assist participants in making decisions, the program clarifies the religious parameters of each tradition and identifies differences in beliefs and practices. Anticipate questons and be prepared to give accurate Jewish and Christian information on the following issues:

* the meaning of Jesus for both Jews and Christians

* explaining Jesus to children

* the Messiah

* life after death

* birth rituals

* religious services

* the Reform Movement's position on intermarriage

Partners often feel uncomfortable attending religious services in their loved ones' house of worship. Discussing these issues can help participants reveal latent feelings and clarify their religious identity.

An issue which will undoubtedly arise is the Reform Movement's position on intermarriage. Be prepared to describe the variety of Reform rabbis' positions regarding officiation at intermarriage. (see appendix 2) Explain why the Reform Movement is not being hypocritical by rejecting intermarriage, but accepting and welcoming intermarried couples and family into the Jewish community.

The issue of officiation at weddings will raise general questions about wedding ceremonies and lead to discussions about couples' wedding plans. Often participants express frustration and anger about certain in-laws, rabbis, and even congregants' responses, occasionally extending their animosity to the entire Jewish community. Discussion of officiation can become quite heated. Prevent this issue from monopolizing the group by talking about religious identity and the benefits of being part of a community. Help participants articulate their expectations in joining the Jewish community.

II. Family and Friends

Much discussion is devoted to the pressures family and friends create for intermarried couples. Sharing experiences can trigger new ideas and strategies. Stress that family attitudes and behaviors can change and that, given time, people often learn to relate more positively to difficult situations. Participants should always remain open to communication with family and friends.

III. Childrearing

The most pressing issue to be discussed is childrearing. Some questions that will be raised include:

* Should we expose our child to both religions and let him/her choose?

* Should we practice no religion in the home?

* Must we choose one religion?

* Will choosing one religion create a situation in which one partner "wins" and the other "loses"?

Encourage all participants to voice their strategies for childrearing and allow group members to challenge each position. The program's position is that couples should choose one religious tradition to predominate in the home. However, since many couples enter the program not wanting to select one religion, you will hear a number of strategies which avoid the need to choose, among them:

* Raising the child equally in both religions and, at a later point, allowing the child to choose.

* Raising a boy in the father's religion and a girl in the mother's.

* Raising the first child in one religion and the next child in the other.

* Raising the child Jewish or Christian depending upon the ethnic composition of the family's hometown or the proximity of specific family members.

Some couples enter the program committed to raising their children as Jews but are troubled by the implications of excluding the religion of the other parent: the non-Jewish parent's feelings of being excluded or invisible in the family and the sense of loss in not passing on his/her own heritage. In such cases, be prepared to validate the feeling of apprehension while also suggesting positive ways for the non-Jewish parent to maintain a sense of individual religious integrity while the child is raised as a Jew. One strategy is

for the non-Jewish parent to celebrate holidays in the home of a parent or family member.
In that way, the opportunity for connectedness is maintained without introducing
non-Jewish symbols or celebrations into the Jewish home. Children can be told that,
whereas we celebrate Chanukah because our home is Jewish, we can help celebrate
Christmas at grandma or grandpa's because we like to be together as a family at such
festive times.

When discussing the reasons for raising children in a single religious tradition,
refer to the discussion of Judaism as a civilization. (see page 32) While it may be
theoretically possible to teach the child by taking the best of each spouse's religion,
Jewish civilization defies such a mixture, since the intertwining strands of religion,
peoplehood, language, history, and ethnicity combine to make Judaism. Pose the following
questions:

* Is it possible to be simultaneously included in and excluded from the Jewish
people?

* Can a group member be accepted by other group members if he/she also
participates in another religious tradition? Can a person affirm Christ and be a
Jew?

* Should the decision of raising a child in both religions be based upon what is best
for the parents or what is best for the child?

Remind the group that the focal point of the discussion is to clarify each partner's
religious attachment and priorities before making decisions about the child's religious
identity. Gently persuade each person to evaluate his/her religious tradition and
determine specifically what should be preserved and why.

IV. Holiday Celebration

Closely related to the discussion of childrearing is the question of holiday celebration. Couples face many decisions:

* What holidays should be celebrated and why?

* Should Christmas and Chanukah, Easter and Passover all be celebrated in the home?

* What religious symbols should be in the home year-round (mezuzah, cross, religious artwork, etc.)?

The program's position is clear: Since we encourage couples to choose one religious tradition for the home, hopefully Judaism, we also encourage them to celebrate only Jewish holidays in the home.

Many couples might be willing to celebrate only Jewish holidays in the home with the exception of Christmas. Christmas is often synonymous with family togetherness, gift-giving, good times, and good food, and may represent all that is beautiful in the Christian partner's family upbringing. Because little religious or theological significance is ascribed to the observance, many couples decide to have a Christmas tree and celebrate the holiday as a secular occasion.

Group discussions should focus on clarifying participants' feelings about celebrating Christmas or Chanukah in the home and exploring their religious identification. Most Jewish partners will express ambivalence or opposition to having a tree, though some may find it acceptable and even desirable.

It is important to stress the critical role of religious symbols in the development of religious identity. Because religious symbols stand for a particular religion, they generate powerful feelings. One religion does not appropriate the religious symbols of another; to do so would devalue them.

Times and Seasons

Part II: Session by Session Outline

Session 1

Session 2

Session 3

Sessions 4-6

Session 7

Session 8: The Shabbat Dinner

Times and Seasons

Times and Seasons

Session 1

Objectives:

    1. To meet participants and begin the group in a warm, supportive environment.

    2. To set "Times and Seasons" within the context of the Outreach effort of Reform Judaism.

    3. To clarify major goals of the program and group expectations for the next eight weeks.

Preparation:

    1. Arrange chairs in a circle.

    2. Set up coffee and refreshments.

    3. Write name tags in large, block letters.

A. Welcome:

    1. Greet participants and ask each person to put on a name tag.

    2. When everyone is present, formally welcome group members.

    3. Give a brief background sketch of the UAHC, the Commission on Reform Jewish Outreach, and the "Times and Seasons" program. (see appendix 3)

B. Introduction:

Provide a short overview of the program:

Times and Seasons

1. This group experience is designed to clarify important issues faced by intermarried couples and couples contemplating intermarriage.

2. There is absolutely no overt or covert attempt to convert the non-Jewish partner. However, the program is sponsored by a Jewish organization; there is no priest or minister sharing the leadership of the group.

3. The program does aim to encourage you to <u>consider</u> creating a Jewish home together and raising your children as Jews.

4. There is no set curriculum to teach about Judaism or intermarriage. Rather, you, the group participants, will provide the agenda by raising the major questions and issues you face as individuals and as couples.

5. As group facilitator, I will provide basic information about Jewish customs and beliefs when appropriate. Those of you who are not Jewish are still connected to the Jewish people through marriage or impending marriage, and it is important for you to understand this community.

6. Although couples are often most interested in talking about their child's religious identity, this will not be the starting point for discussion. Before parents decide what meaning religion should have in their child's life, they should clarify the role of religion in their own. Therefore, before discussing childrearing, the program aims to help you better understand your personal involvement in your own religious tradition.

7. We plan to discuss many sensitive, complicated, explosive, and anxiety-producing

issues in order to strenghten your relationship. Usually these issues are ignored by couples because they disrupt the status quo. When they are broached, often one partner becomes frustrated, defensive, or angry and communication breaks down; or habitually the conversation reaches the same dead end. Using the group as a supportive and constructive challenger, we hope that the quality of your dialogue will improve.

8. There will be seven group sessions and one concluding evening at someone's home, preferably a Shabbat dinner, when we can be less formal and acquaint ourselves with Shabbat. At a later meeting, we will make arrangements for the dinner.

9. No clear-cut solutions should be expected from the program. The group should stimulate continued conversation and communication between partners.

C. Personal experiences:

Explain that the effectiveness of the group depends on the ability of its members to share attitudes and feelings. All participants should feel free to express their opinions. Everyone's ideas are equally valued, and everyone will benefit from the experience and perspective of other group members.

Ask each person to discuss briefly:

1. Growing-up years, family life, religious involvement as a child, significant religious experiences.

2. College years and beyond.

3. Meeting your loved one.

4. The meaning of love in your relationship. (Why do you love him/her? What is it about him/her which convinces you to spend your life together?)

5. The issue of religion in the relationship. (At what point in your relationship did the issue of religion arise? Why did it surface?)

6. Your goals and expectations in the program.

Note: As facilitator, you play a key role in these introductions. To put people at ease, start the process by introducing yourself. If participants feel awkward or embarrassed and give a terse self-introduction, respond by posing questions or pursuing interesting side issues, keeping the discussion light-hearted and enjoyable. Be insistent, not letting anyone off the hook; know at the same time how far to prod and when to stop. Allocate time so that each person has a roughly equal amount of time to speak; otherwise, later in the evening the introductions will be rushed and participants may feel shortchanged. Mention that the sessions usually conclude by 9:30 pm.

D. Break:

There should be a 5-minute break for refreshments and mingling one hour into all group sessions.

E. Closure:

1. Explain "car talk." In the car on the way home, participants should react to what they discussed that evening. This "car talk" will serve as the opening of each week's session.

2. Call on a volunteer to try to remember everyone's name. This is a light-hearted way to conclude and helps reinforce everyone's familiarity with the names.

-28-

3. Ask for a volunteer to bring refreshments to the next session. The synagogue will usually provide coffee and cups.

Session 2

Objectives:

    1. To prepare a list of issues for discussion throughout the remaining sessions. (see appendix 4)

    2. To generate specific questions about Judaism/Christianity.

    3. To discuss Judaism as a religious civilization.

Preparation:

    1. Bring lined paper, pens, a set of Jewish Home pamphlets for each couple, and a roster of group members' name, addresses, and telephone numbers. (see appendix 5)

    2. Read the article "Marriage of Christians and Jews" by Ronald Osborne. (see appendix 6)

A. Car Talk:

    1. Remind the group that "car talk" represents participants' reactions to last week's meeting—what did people talk about on the way home and what issues arose during the week.

    2. Ask for volunteers to report on car talk.

Note: Exercise judgement on car talk time. At times, car talk can lead to relevant, interesting discussions; otherwise, discussion should be kept short. Do not discuss childrearing during the first three sessions.

Times and Seasons

B. Developing the Times and Seasons Agenda:

    1. Distributing lined paper and pens, ask each participant to list the specific issues, concerns, and problems which he/she wants to discuss during the group sessions. Stress that these lists will be anonymous, giving participants the opportunity to ask difficult and embarrassing questions. Encourage people to take their time and write as many questions as they wish.

    2. Collect the lists randomly to ensure anonymity.

C. Jewish/Christian Information:

This approach will help participants learn about Jewish customs, rituals, and holidays. Aspects of Christianity will also be discussed whenever relevant. (see appendix 1)

    1. Elicit specific questions from participants regarding Jewish beliefs, rituals, customs, and holidays. Record all questions on the blackboard.

    2. If the group fails to mention the Holocaust and Israel, add these issues to the list, explaining that they are significant to the Jewish people; no one marrying a Jew should be unclear about the meaning of the Holocaust and Israel for Jews today.

    3. Ask each participant to choose one topic from the list for a thought-starter. Partners should select different issues. Thought-starters should be brief and simple, explaining the participant's personal connection to the issue. The goal is to enable each person to understand his/her thoughts and feelings. Reccomend that participants utilize The Jewish Home, which will be distributed to each couple at the end of the

session, and suggest other relevant resource material for each participant.

4. Depending upon the eagerness of the group to prepare their thought-starters and the number of participants, suggest either that all topics be prepared for the following week or that one or two topics be presented each week.

D. What Does It Mean to Be Jewish?:

Explain that this topic is intended to clarify the meaning of Judaism. The following presentation represents the facilitator's understanding of Judaism and will not necessarily be shared by all Jews. However, by learning what Judaism means to most Jews, the non-Jewish partner will better understand his/her loved one.

1. The Western world has incorrectly defined Judaism as a religion as Christianity, Islam, and Buddhism are defined; Judaism is both a religion and a culture/civilization.

2. A civilization is comprised of many components, most importantly: people, land, language, culture, history, theology, ritual, literature, cuisine. Viewed this way, religion is only one part of the larger Jewish civilization--and not always the most significant part for every Jew. (For more information, see Mordecai Kaplan's Judaism as a Civilization.)

3. Seeing Judaism as a civilization helps us to understand the inconsistencies we observe in individual Jews who possess a strong Jewish identity, feel connected to Judaism and the Jewish people, but are not religiously observant. Some Jews express their Judaism through cultural, social, even culinary means and not primarily

through worship and ritual.

4. Being aware of Judaism as a civilization enables us to understand the meaning of Peoplehood in Jewish life. Peoplehood, comprised of both religion and ethnicity, has played an important part in the Jewish historical experience.

For most of their history (except the last century or two), Jews were separated from the larger non-Jewish world, living in a closed, autonomous society governed by Jewish law and self-regulated by Jewish communal institutions. Certain primary Jewish laws and customs, such as kashrut (dietary regulations), ritual dress, and observances, helped to support the cohesiveness and distinctiveness of the Jewish community; anti-Semitism served to maintain the separateness of Jew and Gentile.

Today, most of these internal and external barriers have disappeared. Jews dress, eat, speak, and grow up in the same environment as non-Jews; Jews and non-Jews work together, date one another, fall in love, and marry. In fact, Jews and non-Jews from similar socioeconomic backgrounds often have more in common than liberal Jews have in common with Orthodox Jews.

5. Viewing Judaism as a civilization allows Jewish participants to evaluate their identity in a new context and helps non-Jews understand the feelings of their loved ones and those who create discomfort in their lives. This does not justify such antagonistic behavior; it may help explain the sense of being an "outsider" experienced by many non-Jews around Jewish family members.

6. Ask for questions and/or reactions during key points in the presentation.

<u>Times and Seasons</u>

Note: Be sure to refer back to this discussion of Judaism as a civilization whenever group discussion focuses on childrearing and taking the "best of both religions." Participants may find it difficult to accept that Judaism cannot be viewed solely as a belief system, like Christianity; it will be necessary to remind the group that Judaism is much broader than a system of belief.

E. <u>Closure</u>:

1. Distribute roster and <u>Jewish Home</u> pamphlets. (see appendix 5)

2. Remind participants to prepare their thought-starters and to remember their car talk.

3. Assign another couple to bring refreshments.

Times and Seasons

Session 3

Objectives:

    1. To explore the meaning of the Holocaust and Israel for group members and for all

Jews.

    2. To discuss issues previously suggested by participants.

    3. To set the date for the Shabbat dinner.

Preparation:

Last week's discussion questions should be typed, double spaced, with no differentiation

between lists, and entitled, "The Times and Seasons Issues for Discussion." (see appendix

4) Bring xeroxed copies of the list for each participant, keeping extra copies on hand in

case participants forget theirs in subsequent weeks.

A. Car Talk

B. Israel and the Holocaust:

The topics of Israel and the Holocaust can be discussed as a unit. Stress the █████████

issues:

    1. The non-Jewish partner needs to understand the legacy of the Holocaust. It was a

trauma inflicted on Jews, a collective assault which is remembered by all Jews,

whether or not they personally lost relatives in the Shoah. The Holocaust forces Jews

to remember a long tradition of oppression and anti-Semitism, much of which was

fostered by the Church (only in 1965 did Vatican II formally exonerate Jews from the charge of killing Jesus). The Holocaust reminds Jews of being separate and different, evoking intense feelings in many Jews, some of whom have little trust in the non-Jewish world (including former Israeli Prime Minister Menachem Begin). Discuss how the "nature of Judaism" causes an entire People to remember the Holocaust, to vow to preserve the memory of the victims, and to ensure that such a tragedy never happens again.

2. The ashes of the Holocaust gave birth to the State of Israel. Without question, the world granted Israel its existence out of sympathy for the death of millions of Jews. For most Jews, Israel is a tremendous source of pride and symbolizes commitment to the future.

3. By marrying a Jew, a non-Jew becomes connected to both the tragedy of the Holocaust and the promise of the State of Israel. Encourage couples to discuss the following issues: Do/should Jews support Israel unconditionally? How should a non-Jewish spouse react when Israel is criticized at a social gathering?

C. Discussion Questions:

Ask participants to read and respond to "The Times and Seasons Issues for Discussion" they created last week. Given the profundity of issues discussed earlier in the evening, you may wish to select for discussion an uncomplicated issue or related issues.

D. Closure:

1. Set a date and place for the Shabbat dinner. This should take place approximately 3-4 weeks after the seventh session in order to give participants time to evaluate the group experience. Ask a couple to volunteer to create the Shabbat dinner in their home. All couples should bring a part of the meal so that the burden of doing everything does not fall on the volunteering couple.

2. Remind participants to prepare their thought-starters for next week.

3. Select a couple to bring refreshments.

Times and Seasons

Sessions 4-6

Objectives:

    1. To explore participants' discussion questions.

    2. To evaluate and clarify group members' personal connection to their religious traditions.

    3. To discuss the Reform Movement's position and programs for welcoming intermarried couples.

Preparation:

Select themes for discussion in sessions 4-6 in the following progression:

    1. General issues related to the meaning of Judaism, ritual celebrations, etc.

    2. The role of family and friends in the life of the intermarried couple.

    3. Children's religious identity.

    4. Holiday celebrations.

These themes will overlap and no session will focus exclusively on one issue. Children's religious identity will most likely dominate sessions 5, 6, and 7.

A. Car Talk

B. Discussion Questions

C. Closure:

    1. Highlight issues planned for the coming session.

    2. Ask another couple to bring refreshments.

Session 7

Objectives:

    1. To give participants a sense of closure.

    2. To assign responsibilities for the Shabbat dinner.

Preparation:

    1. Summarize the various issues discussed in previous sessions. Be ready to present the summary to the group.

    2. Bring evaluation forms. (see appendix 10)

A. Car Talk

B. Wrap Up:

    1. Summarize the issues discussed during the group.

    2. Invite participants to share their feelings about concluding the program, commenting on the group's progress and their own unresolved issues. Couples are often concerned about leaving so much unresolved, so be sure to add that such issues are rarely solved; rather, the group has been a starting point for discussions which will continue for many years.

    3. Encourage participants to raise any remaining questions. Clarify positions on ambiguous or controversial issues.

4. Explore with the group options for maintaining contact in the future, perhaps by meeting monthly as a <u>chavurah</u>, getting together for major holidays, or appointing a guest speaker to address the group from time to time on issues of interest. Specific plans for follow-up meetings must be established during this session and the following Shabbat dinner.

5. Finalize plans for the Shabbat dinner. Remind participants about the time and place, and decide what each couple will bring.

6. Distribute evaluations for participants to complete. (see appendix 10)

Times and Seasons

Session 8: The Shabbat Dinner

Objectives:

1. To experience Shabbat together.

2. To explore possibilities for follow-up.

3. To discuss any unfinished business.

Preparation:

1. Provide reference sheets of the Shabbat blessings printed in transliteration as well as in translation and basic instructions on preparing for Shabbat.

2. Order a "Do It Yourself Shabbat" from the UAHC publication catalogue for each couple.

A. The Dinner:

1. Briefly explain the Shabbat dinner rituals. The evening should be primarily social in nature.

2. Invite participants to join in the blessing over the candles, wine, and challah.

3. Encourage the sharing of family memories of Shabbat.

4. Make specific plans for future meetings.

Times and Seasons

Appendices

Experimental
Educational
Editions

JEWS and CHRISTIANS:

teaching about each other

A MANUAL FOR TEACHERS

Part 2: Guidelines for Religious Educators

edited by
Lawrence McCoombe
and Annette Daum

UNION of AMERICAN HEBREW CONGREGATIONS
NEW YORK

SOME SENSITIVE ISSUES: PERSPECTIVES, PROBLEMS, POSSIBILITIES

ANNETTE DAUM, Coordinator of the Department of Interreligious
Affairs, Union of American Hebrew Congregations

LAWRENCE McCOOMBE, Chairman, Commission on Christian-Jewish
Relations, Diocese of Long Island (Episcopal)

Guidelines for Religious Educators

Before we begin to focus on specific sensitive topics, we offer a few
broad guidelines in the form of "don'ts." These are directed toward
correcting general approaches and attitudes that breed misunderstanding
of each other. We present these suggestions here for two reasons:
1) Most of them are quite general in application and so are relevant
to several topics; 2) Some concern topics that are not dealt with at
all in the treatments that follow.

The guidelines are in negative form because interreligious relationships could be enhanced significantly if we were simply to stop teaching certain things about each other.

What Jews Should Not Teach About Christians

1. Do not teach that all Christian denominations think that they have
    the only "true" religion, or that only Christians hold such a view.
    (What about Orthodox Jews?)

2. Do not teach that all Christian bodies preach Christianity as the
    only way to salvation.

3. Do not teach that Christian belief is concerned only with the life-
    to-come (after death).

4. Do not compare modern Judaism with ancient Christianity in order to
    develop a sense that Judaism is sophisticated and realistic and
    Christianity simple and otherworldly. Compare instead first
    century Judaism with first century Christianity, modern Judaism
    with modern Christianity.

5. Do not teach that Christianity is a missionary religion, while
    Judaism is not. When they study Jewish history, students should
    learn that there were times when Judaism was a strongly missionizing
    religion. Moreover, students should be made aware that only some
    segments of fundamentalist Protestantism cooperate with prosely-
    tizing groups like Jews for Jesus, and that not only Jews, but main-
    line Protestants and Roman Catholics as well, are threatened by
    increasing missionary efforts on the part of fundamentalist
    Christians and cult groups.

6. Do not teach, whether overtly or by omission, that only Jews died
    in the Holocaust. Mention those Christians who died and those who
    tried to save Jewish lives.

7. Do not teach the content of the Christian gospels without intro-
    ducing the current statements on deicide -- the Roman Catholic
    statements, Episcopal statements and the Vatican Guidelines.

8. Do not leave the impression with students that Jews were the only
    people ever to have been persecuted because of religious beliefs.

9. Do not teach that our only relationships with Christians have
    always been bad.

10. Do not teach your own interpretations of Christian theology as if
    they were the "facts" about Christianity.

11. Do not teach that only Jews support Israel. Use Episcopal and
    other Christian statements as well.

What Christians Should Not Teach About Jews

1. Do not teach that Law and Commandment are narrow, negative or
    limited.

2. Do not teach Jesus' quotations of Hebrew Scripture as if they ori-
    ginated with him.

3. Do not teach the Holocaust as if it were a Christian experience,
    omitting the crucial point that Hitler's aim was the destruction
    of all Jews. Christians were not killed for being Christians. Jews
    were killed for being Jews.

4. Do not lump anti-Semitism with other forms of prejudice, e.g., against
    Blacks or Hispanics. Because of the very special relationship
    between Christianity and Judaism, anti-Semitism has theological
    roots and should be handled separately.

5. Do not leave students with the impression that Judaism disappeared
    with the coming of Jesus, or that Jewish ties to the land of Israel
    disappeared with the fall of the Temple in the year 70 A.D.

6. Do not compare modern Christianity with ancient Judaism in order to
    develop a sense that Christianity is sophisticated and realistic
    and Judaism primitive and burdensome. Compare instead first century
    Christianity with first century Judaism, modern Christianity with
    modern Judaism.

7. Do not teach sensitive gospel materials (the Passion, the Pharisees, the controversy accounts) without commentary to place these materials in proper perspective.

8. Do not teach that Christianity alone is a religion of love, while Judaism is a religion of law, that the God of the Hebrew Scripture is vengeful and warlike and the New Testament God is gracious and good, etc.

9. Do not present Judaism as a monolithic entity without a variety of observances and emphases.

MESSIAH

(A Jewish Perspective)

On the subject of the Messiah, Judaism and Christianity face each other over an unbridgeable gulf. Jews and Christians view the concept of "messiah" from different perspectives: a crucial difference that is as irreconcilable today as it was 2000 years ago.

"Messiah" is a Greek word, originally translated from a Hebrew word, which means "the anointed one." In early days, mashiach was not a proper name but a term referring to those men who were consecrated to high office, such as kings and high priests, in a ceremony which consisted of special benedictions accompanied by the pouring of the holy oil on their heads.

In the years following the Babylonian Exile, about 700 years before the birth of Jesus, Jews began to long for a Messiah, a leader who would restore them to their former greatness and independence in their home-land. There, the Temple would be rebuilt, and sacrificial worship rein-stituted. There were many different views of the Messiah in Judaism, ranging from the natural to the mystical. Both natural and mystical expectations of the Messiah, of what would happen in "the days of the Messiah," are found in the Hebrew Bible and other Jewish literature. Almost all would agree that the Messiah would be a descendant of King David, a military and political leader -- a human being, like Moses. This Messiah would be a messenger from God. His arrival would be an-nounced by the Prophet Elijah and would be immediately preceded by war, starvation and unbelievable oppression. His coming would then usher in a new society where God's kingdom would be established on earth, an age in which all people would live together in peace and justice.

By the time of Roman rule, conditions had become so intolerable that longing for the coming of the Messiah gained momentum. But Jesus did not meet Jewish criteria for the long-awaited Messiah. He was neither the great military or political leader they expected; nor did he usher in an age of universal peace and justice. His crucifixion would have been regarded as a defeat and thus a sure sign that this was not the Messiah.

By the second century C.E., many Jews were still expecting the imminent coming of a Messiah, but it was Bar Kochba, the leader of the uprising in 132-135 C.E. who was thought of in those terms now, not Jesus. Jesus was not the only man to be thought of as the Messiah; among others in Jewish history, Jacob Frank and Sabbetai Tzvi were also mistakenly viewed as being messiahs by groups of Jews after the time of Jesus.

While traditional Jews today are still waiting for the Messiah, students should learn that Reform Jews no longer expect the coming of a personal messiah, but seek to work in partnership with God to establish a messi-anic age of peace, justice and righteousness for all people here on earth, when

> "...they shall beat their swords into plowshares,
> And their spears into pruning-hooks,
> Nation shall not lift up sword against nation,
> Neither shall they learn war anymore."

(Isaiah 2:4)

MESSIAH

(A Christian Perspective)

"Christians believe that Jesus was the Messiah. Jews don't." This statement has been, at best, the font of much misunderstanding over the years. At worst, it has been one of the primary sources of Christian anti-Semitism.

The Christian concept of Messiah as the dying and rising Son of God is very different from the Messiah in Jewish expectation. The earliest Christians had to alter, stretch and reinterpret their own expectations in order to apply the title to Jesus (cf. Luke 24:13-27). He simply does not appear to have accomplished what was expected of the Messiah by the great majority of his own people in his own time and place.

The earliest Christians, of course, did apply the title to Jesus. But when they spoke of him in this way, they transformed the content of that title to reflect their religious experience and belief about the saving significance of his death and resurrection. The title "Messiah" used by Christians had quickly come to mean something radically different from the same title as it was used by most Jews. From that early time until the present, Christian teaching has tended to portray Jesus' own people as being so spiritually blind that they could not perceive the "obvious" fact that he was God's anointed.

If we Christians are to speak with integrity about Jesus as Messiah, we ought to begin by acknowledging that we have appropriated the title from Judaism and given it radical reinterpretation in light of the early Christian experience of the death, resurrection and ascension of Jesus. "Jesus is Messiah" will then be recognized as a statement of Christian faith and not one of empirical fact which Jews are simply too stubborn or dense to accept.

MESSIAH: PROBLEMS AND POSSIBILITIES

(A Joint Perspective)

Problems

1. Christians should not gloss over their responsibility for the teachings of the Church regarding Jewish rejection of Jesus as the Messiah, a rejection which has been used all too often to justify Jewish suffering.

2. Some Christians reflect a grave misunderstanding in their premise that Jews simply need to be shown that Jesus was the awaited Messiah in order to be converted to Christianity. In fact, Jewish and Christian concepts of the Messiah represent irreconcilable differences. These ideas are not open to empirical proof, but are matters of faith and belief. They must be accepted as such by each group.

3. The interreligious dimension of this topic is dealt with most directly in the classroom when Christians speak of the Jews' "rejection" of Jesus as Messiah. Some Christian teachers say simply and patronizingly, "How sad!" Others teach that Jewish suffering throughout history has resulted from this rejection. Neither of these attitudes acknowledges the integrity of Judaism as a living and licit religion.

4. The Church has always tested and substantiated (for the faithful) the claim that Jesus is Messiah by referring to prophecies embodied in the Hebrew Scripture. But this is a very different enterprise from claiming that those prophets "forecast" the coming of Jesus the Messiah, or that these Scriptures prove in any rationally defensible way Jesus' exclusive right to that title. In short, both Jews and Christians need to realize that, while Jesus' messiahship may be illuminated by Hebrew Scripture, it cannot be demonstrated thereby without mistranslating or misunderstanding.

Possibilities

1. Churches should have seminars on curricula. These should include information about modern Jews and Judaism, so that the children gain a concept of Judaism's depth, richness and vitality. Judaism would not then be mistaught as simply legalism or as a religion that is the same as Christianity, only without Jesus.

2. Both Jewish and Christian religious schools should have courses on comparative religion.

3. Both Jews and Christians should teach that Jesus and his disciples were Jewish.

WHO KILLED JESUS?

(A Jewish Perspective)

The charge of deicide has haunted the Jewish people for the last 2000 years. Gospel accounts, which were composed during 65-100 C.E., place primary responsibility for the death of Jesus on the Jews, and have been used as an excuse to foster anti-Semitism ever since.

Most modern scholars, Jewish and Christian, would agree that Jesus was arrested, tried, and sentenced, and executed in the Roman manner by Roman authorities, that he was regarded as a political rebel and a threat to Roman rule because he claimed to be "king of the Jews." Since the trial narrative was not written from an historical perspective as we understand it today, it is inconsistent with the little that is known of that period from sources other than the New Testament.

Jesus' trial before the Sanhedrin could not have happened as described in the New Testament, because the regular assembly met during the day and was never convened at night on the Sabbath, on Jewish holidays, or on the day preceding the Sabbath or a holiday. Meeting the night before a holiday and reaching a verdict of guilty on the first day of a trial, punishment by crucifixion -- all would have been in violation of Jewish law. Many safeguards in Jewish law made it so difficult that a Sanhedrin which issued as much as single death penalty in seven years was regarded as bloody. It was also unlikely that the Sanhedrin would turn over a Jew to Roman authorities to be killed. If such a "court" did meet, as described in the New Testament, it could not have been the regular Sanhedrin. It would have been a kangaroo court, perhaps a handful of wealthy Jews anxious to cooperate with Roman authorities in disposing of a threat.

Historians also record that Pontius Pilate slaughtered Galileans and Samaritans with impunity. Since he was known for his violent and cruel treatment of people, his portrait in the Gospels is unrealistic and incompatible with fact. While no one can state with certainty the reasons for this account, it is likely that responsibility for the death of Jesus was shifted from Pilate for political purposes, to allay the suspicion of the Roman authorities regarding Christians. Placing responsibility for deicide on the Jews would also serve a theological purpose, for the message of the New Testament was now directed toward gaining converts from the pagan world.

Since to this day Jewish children are still being accused of deicide, this unit is taught from an historical perspective, and designed to provide students with basic information regarding the death of Jesus so that they may be able to respond to the ancient charge. New textbooks and instructional material are now available to help Jewish students realize that some Christian bodies such as the Episcopal Church and the Roman Catholic Church have issued statements rejecting the charge of deicide against the Jews and condemning anti-Semitism. Proper use of this information in both Jewish and Christian religious schools represents a necessary preliminary step towards eliminating centuries of prejudice and mistrust.

WHO KILLED JESUS?

(A Christian Perspective)

Jews care deeply about this question and about the historically per-
sistent Christian answer that lays the blame at every Jewish door.

Many clergy avoid the historical question by transfering the matter into
the realm of theology, emphasizing that all humanity is responsible for
the death of Jesus, that this death was sacrificial and redemptive, that
on the cross we see not Jesus in trouble, but God in action, and so on.
They seem far more concerned with discussing the theological significance of Jesus' death than answering the basic questions, Who put Jesus
to death, and why? While the theological questions may be primary,
however, the historical questions are prior.

Part of the Christian reluctance to face the historical questions stems
from the fact that many clergy are unaware or unaccepting of the
scholarly consensus that Jesus was put to death by the Roman government
and that Jewish complicity in the matter, if any, was limited to the
Sadducean party and the Temple officials.

The result of this reluctance has been the continued public reading of
the passion narratives with no comment on their historical reliability
-- narratives which portray the Jews as a dull, self-interested, evil
mob who would crucify God's own Son. And this reading has, in turn,
fueled the opportunistic and politically expedient fires of anti-
Semitism.

WHO KILLED JESUS? PROBLEMS AND POSSIBILITIES

(A Joint Perspective)

Problems

1. The thrust of Jewish teaching on this subject will be to instruct the children in how to defend themselves against deicide charges. Christian teaching will focus on the significance of Jesus' death as the act of God, reconciling the world to himself.

2. Jews should not blame their Christian neighbors in America today for what happened in Europe during centuries of persecution undergone because of deicide charges.

3. The statements on deicide issued by the Episcopal Diocese of Long Island, the Episcopal Church and the Second Vatican Council should be used by both Christian and Jewish teachers to set the twentieth century record straight.

4. The reading of the Gospel accounts literally and without comment could continue to reinforce the ancient deicide charge.

Possibilities

1. The trial and crucifixion narratives should be presented, interpreted and understood with historical explanation. Make it clear that the gospels were not intended as unbiased or as purely historical accounts in our modern sense, and that Jews are not guilty of deicide.

2. Explain that Jesus was born, lived and died a faithful Jew, that his message was directed toward Jews. Emphasize the fact that all of the apostles and all of the earliest Christians were Jews. "One of the tragic things that may be said about the history of the western world is that we are likely to remember the Jews as the people who killed Jesus. We might better remember the Jews as the people who produced Jesus." (Theodore Parker Ferris)

3. Potential anti-Semitism, whether grounded in deicide charges or other sources, needs to be informed by Jesus' own echoing of the law of his people: Love your neighbor as yourself.

HOLIDAYS

(A Jewish Perspective)

Jewish holidays are celebrated on three different levels -- as nature festivals or in commemoration of great historical events and in affirmation of the place of God in Jewish history.

Jewish festivals are family-oriented and are usually celebrated in the house and the synagogue. While customs and ceremonies may vary, tzedakah -- the giving of money or other aid to people in need -- is an integral part of every celebration.

Passover is the archetypal Jewish holiday. It is the oldest and one of the most important Jewish holidays, for it marks the birth of the Jews as a free people and a nation over 3000 years ago. Passover originated as a shepherd festival, celebrated long before the Exodus. Elements of a later agricultural festival were added and then incorporated into the observances. After the Exodus, Pesach was reinterpreted as a joyous festival of the Jewish people to be celebrated in remembrance of their redemption from spiritual and physical bondage in Egypt. While Passover is associated with a particular event in the history of the Jews, universalist concepts are added and the holiday is also celebrated to remind us that our freedom to serve God obligates us to fight for the freedom of all people.

A central part of the celebration is the reading of the Haggadah, which takes place at the family Seder. Although the Seder is a ceremony that takes place in the home, it is nevertheless a religious experience which serves to reaffirm belief in a God who is sensitive to the suffering of all people.

Since the Haggadah has never been canonized, original poems and stories, illustrations as well as prayers for the future, may be added and incorporated into the ceremony. In modern times, a special prayer has been inserted called the Matzah of Hope. It concerns the plight of Soviet Jewry and is recited as a reminder that we must fight for the physical and spiritual freedom of our fellow Jews in the Soviet Union today. After the Matzah of Hope, not only do we pray for Jews, but traditionally for all who are in want. The Haggadah states, "Let all who are hungry come and eat. Let all who are in want share the hope of Passover..."

A special issue of Keeping Posted, a UAHC magazine for religious school students, was devoted to the subject of hunger in the world, and was used to encourage tzedakah projects of aid to the poor all over the world. Another ritual incorporated into the Seder in modern times is the ritual of remembrance for the six million Jews who perished at the hands of the Nazis during the Holocaust. This ceremony is conducted to remind us that tyranny is not ancient history and must still be fought in modern times.

The Seder concludes with the singing of L'shana haba-ah b'Yerushalayim -- next year in Jerusalem -- because the return to Jerusalem has been part of the hope of the Jewish people since the destruction of the Second Temple by the Romans in 70 C.E. With the conclusion of the Seder, we are left with the challenge to use the opportunity of freedom to bring the messianic era about in our time here on earth.

HOLIDAYS

(A Christian Perspective)

The observance of special days and seasons is important to both Judaism and Christianity. When Christian holidays commemorate events which happened in a Jewish context, some confusion arises. The Christian festival of Pentecost, for instance, marks a special event in the life of the early Church, the coming of the Holy Spirit upon the gathered disciples. The Christian festival is called Pentecost because this event took place during the celebration of the Jewish feast of the same name.

An even closer relationship exists between the events of Holy Week/ Easter -- Maundy Thursday, Good Friday and Easter Day -- and Passover. Not only did they originally coincide temporally, but their meanings were seen by the Church to be closely related. In fact, the word for Easter in many languages is still the word for Passover.

Until the late second century C.E., the Eastern churches observed as a single saving event the death/resurrection of Jesus; the observance took place at the same time Jews were observing Passover. Even as early as New Testament times, the crucified and risen Christ was being referred to in Passover terms: "Christ our paschal lamb is sacrificed for us; therefore let us keep the feast." (I Corinthians 5:7)

The Seder, too, took on special significance for Christians, since it is to such a ritual meal that the synoptic gospels trace the institution of the Holy Eucharist.

Not only the rites and symbols, but the very meaning of Passover was taken up by Christians into the Holy Week/Easter celebration; in the passion/resurrection of Christ was the true passage from bondage (sin and death) into freedom (new and eternal life).

Add to these reinterpretations by Christians of certain Jewish festivals the fact that the observance of Christmas has, unfortunately, been allowed in public schools, at least in secularized form, and the result is an unspoken but certainly pervasive Christian triumphalism, which renders Jewish self-perception irrelevant to both culture and Christianity.

HOLIDAYS: PROBLEMS AND POSSIBILITIES

(A Joint Perspective)

Problems

1. Our holidays are not counterparts to each other. Yom Kippur is not "Jewish Good Friday," Chanukah is not "Jewish Christmas," and so on. There should be no attempt to gloss over our real differences.

2. Both Jews and Christians should deal with Christmas as a Christian holiday and not secularize it. The secular input doesn't help. "Christmas is a time for giving," etc., obscures the meaning of this central festival of the Incarnation. The warmhearted, secular notion of Christmas has become so confused with the religious holiday that a whole generation of American children has grown up thinking of "Jingle Bells" and "Rudolph the Red-Nosed Reindeer" as Christmas carols.

3. When we do teach about each other's holidays, we do so only superficially. This is perhaps worse than no teaching at all, for it makes each faith look to the other naive and superstitious. To say, for instance, that Chanukah commemorates the Maccabean rededication of the Temple and leave it at that, misunderstands the meaning of that occasion for Jews. Likewise, to say that Easter celebrates the rising of Jesus from the dead is not enough. The meaning (for believers) of the event celebrated is as important for understanding as the event itself.

4. Too often, when Christian teachers discuss the Last Supper they either omit the key Passover symbols and their meanings, or so reinterpret the symbols from a Christian point of view that the purpose of the Seder for Jews is either dropped entirely or grossly misrepresented. Such approaches strip the Seder of its Jewish meaning and leave Christian children with the unfortunate impression that the Seder and the Eucharist are obviously one and the same.

5. Christians do not understand that their most important holidays, their most joyous celebrations have historically been times of greatest persecution of Jews.

Possibilities

1. Learn about each other's religious holidays and the rites and customs that go with them. (Note: The actual observance of religious holidays does not properly fall into the realm of responsibility of the public schools.)

2. Guidelines should be developed to help Jewish religious school teachers to deal with Christmas with respect while helping students to realize that it is not their holiday.

3. In the context of the freedom festivals of Easter and Passover, Jews and Christians should inform students about Christian support for Soviet Jews.

4. Consider holding an interreligious service commemorating the Holocaust.

5. Christian teachers should attempt to teach the Holocaust as a Jewish experience. Both Christians and Jews should be knowledgeable about those Christians who helped to save Jews during those times.

6. Holiday exchanges between Jewish and Christian religious schools such as an interfaith Seder should be encouraged.

BIBLE STORIES

(A Jewish Perspective)

The Hebrew Bible has profoundly affected the course of human history of western civilization in general and American democracy in particular. Hebrew Scripture serves as the constitution for all branches of Judaism and as a starting point for both Christianity and Islam. Translated into over 900 languages, the Hebrew biblical concepts of God as One, and of morality as expressed in the Ten Commandments were later adopted by Christianity and Islam to form the foundations of religious belief and morality for half the people in the world.

While traditional Jews view the Bible as the word of God, given by God to Moses, liberal Jews view it as a history told by Jews in symbolic, legendary style. All would agree that the Hebrew Bible describes the history of the Jewish people; their religious, social, ethical beliefs and practices; their relationship with God; and their search for understanding of God's will.

Torah, which means "teaching," began as oral history and was transmitted by word of mouth for generations before being recorded on parchment scrolls. While the term Torah is usually applied to the first five books of the Hebrew Bible, it is also commonly used when referring to the entire Hebrew Bible and even to the totality of Jewish law. The standard Hebrew text in use in synagogues today is itself an interpretation produced by the Masoretes in the tenth century C.E. The Masoretic Text is confirmed by the Dead Sea Scrolls which antedate this text by as much as 1200 years. Since no original manuscript is available, and since the oldest parchment scrolls were written several hundred years after they were composed, it is not surprising that different versions of the same story arose and have been incorporated into the text. Since the Hebrew text contains no vowels, biblical scholars even today cannot be sure of the original words in some cases. Additional problems in understanding are presented when the Hebrew text, as developed through the ages, is further interpreted according to the insights of the various translators.

After the Babylonian Exile, Ezra the Scribe began the process of collecting the scrolls of the Jewish people. Over the next 700 years, additional books were written and examined to determine whether they were worthy of inclusion in the Bible, a process which was finally concluded at about 100 C.E. when the rabbis in the Sanhedrin canonized the Hebrew Scriptures for all time.

As canonized, the Hebrew Scriptures contain 39 books divided into three parts:

    I. <u>Torah</u> - Genesis, Exodus, Leviticus, Numbers, Deuteronomy.

II. <u>The Prophets</u> - Joshua, Judges, Samuel I and II, Kings I and II, Isaiah, Jeremiah, Ezekiel, Hosea, Joel, Amos, Abadiah, Jonah, Micah, Nahum, Habakkuk, Zephaniah, Haggai, Zechariah, Malachi.

III. <u>The Writings</u> - Psalms, Proverbs, Job and the Five Megillot (Song of Songs, Esther, Ruth, Lamentations, Ecclesiastes), Dan, Ezra, Nehemiah, Chronicles I and II.

In the mainstream of Jewish thinking, biblical stories such as Creation through Cain and Abel (Genesis 1-4:16) would be interpreted as indicating that God is responsible for all creation and that all creation is good. From the very beginning, human beings were created in the image of God and had free will. As illustrated in the story of the Garden of Eden, the first human beings exercised that free will by disobeying God. Their sin, eating from the Tree of Knowledge, is regarded in Judaism as an act of commission, not a state of being.

While the temptation to sin is always present, human beings, by following God's guidance, have the power to overcome these inclinations. The closing story of the unit, Cain and Abel, which ends in murder, illustrates what happens when people allow their differences to overcome their common humanity. By this act of murder, Cain is banished from society and feels separated from God's protection, a consequence he finds unbearable. Because of Cain's repentance, God mercifully protects him from vengeance. While the legends in this unit may or may not be regarded as literally true, these stories contain a good deal of truth about the nature of both humanity and God.

Perhaps another brief tale can best illustrate the meaning of Torah for Jews. Long ago, a pagan asked the great Rabbi Hillel to explain the essence of Torah while standing on one foot. Hillel's classic reply was, "What is hateful unto yourself, do not do unto others. This is the whole of Torah; all the rest is commentary. Go and study."

BIBLE STORIES

(A Christian Perspective)

Christians and Jews speak of "The Bible" with differing reference. By
"Bible" Jews mean the Hebrew Scriptures, what Christians call the Old
Testament. Christians use "Bible" to mean the Old and New Testaments
taken together.

A summary statement about the origin and authority of the Old and New
Testaments as understood by most of the Church today will provide a helpful backdrop against which to consider our use of Bible stories.

The Hebrew Bible is an anthology of the literature of the people called
Israel. It includes a broad assortment of literary forms and interests:
prose and poetry, hymns and imprecations, folk tales and history,
theology, genealogy, law, advice, apocalyptic, and a special literary
genre called prophecy.

Isolated passages of these Hebrew Scriptures are dated at least as
early as 1700 B.C. Some books were written as late as 150 B.C. Many
of the stories circulated orally for centuries before they were written
down; others were literary productions from the first. All of the
books show evidence of compilation and/or redaction. No authoritative
and exclusive list of these Hebrew books was drawn up until about
A.D. 90, when the rabbinical academy at Jabneh determined a canon of
Scripture.

The New Testament is a collection of some of the literature used by
the early Christian Church. As indicated above, the span covered by
the Hebrew Scriptures is well over a thousand years. The New Testament
books, in contrast, were written in the course of the hundred years
preceding A.D. 150. Again, many literary types are included: letters,
hymns, sermons, creeds, theological history, apocalyptic, treatises,
and a special literary genre called "gospel" -- a form of theological
statement in a biographical style and structure. No universally agreed
upon list of the books that today make up the New Testament appears
until the fourth century A.D. The criteria applied at that time for
inclusion in the canon were essentially two: (1) Did the writing bear
the name of an apostle as author? (2) Was the writing in general use
in the Church? The twenty-seven books of purported apostolic author-
ship which were in general use at the time, especially in the influential
metropolitan churches, had by the year 369 become accepted as the New
Testament, the inspired word of God, equal in authority and inspiration
to the Hebrew Scriptures, the "Old Testament."

Although the canon of the New Testament was settled so many centuries
ago, the nature of biblical authority and inspiration remains a live
issue even today. Within the Episcopal Church alone, a broad variety
of opinion exists. Every priest is required before ordination to
declare that he/she believes the Holy Scriptures to be the Word of
God. Yet there remain among clergy and laity alike many interpretations

of "Word of God," ranging from the belief that the Holy Spirit dictated each word to the belief that the Scriptures are a human account of humanity's perception of the encounter with God in historical events. What we mean by biblical inspiration, and consequently what we mean by biblical authority, varies greatly within the Church.

This discussion of scriptural authority becomes important in connection with Bible stories in the classroom because certain Bible stories have had attached to them over the years (even from earliest Christian times) certain interpretations. Although, strictly speaking, these interpretations belong to the category of "tradition" rather than Scripture, the degree of authority assigned to Scripture has tended to spill over and influence the authority of the interpretation. If, for example, a Christian interprets Abraham's near sacrifice of Isaac (Genesis 22) as a foreshadowing of God's sacrifice of his Son Jesus and if this Christian holds a literalist doctrine of biblical inspiration, assigning a high degree of authority to Scripture, he/she will give to the interpretation the status of revealed truth. Thus does interpretation -- especially traditional interpretation -- become fact.

Further, in traditional Christian usage, a great number of stories and prophecies found in Hebrew Scriptures are seen as types or foreshadowings whose fulfillment is seen in Jesus, the Messiah. Adam's sin, for instance, is dealt with by Jesus, the "second Adam." The paschal lamb is an antetype of Jesus, the Lamb of God. The manna in the desert is a foreshadowing of the bread of the Eucharist. The prophecies of Isaiah point to Jesus.

Such an approach leads inevitably to the conclusion that the Old Testament is promise and the New Testament fulfillment, the Old Testament a record of a disobedient people and the New Testament the beginning of an obedient Israel, the Old Testament a broken covenant, the New a living one. Ultimately this results in the view that Judaism is a dead or invalid religion, that it is perfected, fulfilled and replaced by Christianity. Of all the Hebrew Scriptures, only those remain relevant which somehow point toward the New Covenant. And all of this begins with a view of scriptural authority grounded in a particular doctrine of inspiration.

The place to begin to combat this problem is in the study of history. The doctrine of biblical inspiration is most conservative where knowledge of the history of the biblical text and times is weakest. ("The meanings or patterns discernible in 'history'....are clearest for each of us in the periods he has studied least." - C.S. Lewis)

When we tell children Bible stories, we are building concepts of history, theology, human nature and more. Great care must therefore be taken in interpreting or passing judgment on the personalities, people and events of the Bible. These should be viewed and understood first and foremost in the context and milieu which produced them, without immediate extrapolation into traditional Christian theological interpretations.

Two examples: The story of Adam and Eve and the serpent is not told to explain how the human need for redemption came about. It is about the estranging consequences of disobedience and the freedom of human beings to choose.

The Cain and Abel story of Genesis 4, likewise, is not about the sinfulness of human nature which is to be redeemed in Christ. Nor is it about the necessity of blood sacrifice. Again, it is about human freedom to choose obedience to God and how the choice to disobey God disrupts our relationships with human beings as well. Both of the stories cited deal with obedience, estrangement and punishment.

Prophecy must be allowed to maintain its integrity, too. The "Behold, a virgin shall conceive" prophecy of Isaiah 7:14 should be viewed and understood primarily not as a prophecy fulfilled in Jesus, but as one aspect of the ministry of Isaiah of Jerusalem, a prophecy which had relevance and bearing on Isaiah's own time and place.

Similarly, the institution of the Passover should not be compared with the crucifixion and resurrection of Jesus, unless and until Passover's significance for Jews then and now is rather fully understood.

Only as we understand before we interpret can Christians and Jews point with honesty and integrity to the Bible as a common and shared resource.

BIBLE STORIES: PROBLEMS AND POSSIBILITIES

(A Joint Perspective)

Problems

1. The Bible is not the same collection of books for Jews and Christians. This is not always made clear. Further, even those writings which we hold in common as sacred Scripture are given very different interpretations and emphases by our respective traditions.

2. Some Christian teachers consistently teach faith-knowledge (e.g., that Jesus was the long-promised Messiah) and historical data (e.g., that great crowds came to Jerusalem for Passover) without distinguishing them. This is, of course, presenting an interpretation as a fact.

3. If the Hebrew Scriptures are approached primarily in terms of trinitarian Christian theology, the original intent is already misunderstood.

4. The people of the Bible were Jewish. Yet Christians seldom mention this fact, except when contrasting them with Jesus (as if their Jewishness had something to do with what made them different from Jesus). Our children need to know that Abraham and David -- and Jesus -- were Jewish, too.

Possibilities

1. Upper grades and adults might enjoy an investigation of the literary genres represented in Scripture: legend, saga, myth, history, prophecy, hymn, wisdom literature, etc. An adult interreligious course on the Bible might be offered.

2. Teachers can point out along the way that the main characters in the stories they are recounting are Jewish, that they did not live in a universal and timeless realm, but in a particular time and place, that they have living descendants today, and that these Jews today still teach the concept of the one God and worship that God.

3. In retelling the events of the New Testament, Christian teachers can be careful not to leave the impression that Christians and Jews were separate and distinct in New Testament times. Most of the New Testament was, after all, written by Jews.

4. Where verses in the New Testament are quotations from Hebrew Scriptures, the teacher should acknowledge the original source.

THE PHARISEES

(A Jewish Perspective)

Historically, Judaism at the time of Jesus, as now, was far from monolithic. Socio-economic differences led to religious-political differences, so that the Sadducees, who were the wealthy aristocrats, were
the priestly class who controlled the Sanhedrin. The Pharisees were
the major opposition religious sect that challenged their control.

The Pharisees, who emerged about two centuries before Jesus, are
revered by the Jews as the ancestors of rabbinic Judaism and are
thus more closely allied to all branches of modern Judaism than any
other sect in existence at that time. The word "pharisee" (perushim
in Hebrew) could mean either "those who separated themselves," or
"those who explained." Two words describe the differences between the
parties: literal and liberal. The Sadducees followed the teachings of
Torah literally as written, whereas the Pharisees expanded the Torah
by adding interpretations and explanations which were handed down
orally and applying these to contemporary society. This enabled
Judaism to adapt to changing conditions, and it kept the religion alive.

The Pharisees were the party of the masses whose leaders were scholars,
teachers and scribes. They fostered greater democracy in Judaism by
creating a system that enabled the poor as well as the rich to participate in Temple sacrifices, and founded schools in the synagogues so
that all men, rich and poor, could be knowledgeable about Torah. The
synagogue thus became a major institution where all the people assembled
to learn and to pray. They also preached the concepts of bodily resurrection, thus offering hope to a Jewish people in despair of oppressive
Roman rule. There were different schools of thought within the Pharisaic
community, exemplified by the teachings of Hillel and Shammai. In dis-
pute, both opinions would be kept, but later rabbis were more apt to
be guided by Hillel's more liberal decisions. A few famous quotations
indicate his attitude towards education and towards peace:

> "Do not say, 'I shall study when I have leisure; perhaps you
> will never have the leisure."
> "Love peace, seek peace, love mankind: in this way, lead them
> to the Lord."
> What is hateful unto thee, do not do unto thy neighbor."

Many of the sayings attributed to Jesus in the New Testament are similar
to familiar Pharisaic sayings. When Jesus is asked in the Book of
Matthew, "Is it against the law to cure on the Sabbath?" his answer
is the same as that given by the Pharisees. According to Judaism,
indeed, the law must be broken if it seems to stand in the way of
saving a life. Jews are therefore dismayed at finding the Pharisees
described in such derogatory terms in the New Testament; it is regret-
ful that the word itself has become synonymous with "hypocrite."

After the fall of the Temple in 70 C.E., all other parties, such as the Sadducees and the Essenes, virtually disappeared. The Pharisees then became the majority and the ruling party. Thus, at the time the New Testament was written, Pharisee and Jew were virtually the same, and the Pharisees became the archetype of Jesus' enemies.

THE PHARISEES

(A Christian Perspective)

The Pharisees were the architects of the mainstream of Judaism. Their daily debates on the moral and religious obligations of individual Jews formed the basis for a Judaism which, after the revolt of 66-70 A.D., was forced to continue without the Jerusalem Temple as the unifying force in its identity. The Pharisees, then, are the heroes of the Jewish past, the pioneers of a Judaism which has been able to survive even to today.

The New Testament speaks of the Pharisees one-sidedly and unfairly, but predictably. The Church which produced the gospels was a Jewish sect and, in the eyes of the Pharisees, a perverse one. It is therefore no surprise that the New Testament portrays the Pharisees as hypocritical and legalistic. To the gospel writers, the Pharisees were the enemy. Looking at the teachings of Jesus himself, however, we find that his opinions on several matters reveal him as standing closer ideologically to the Pharisees than to any other religio-political party of his day.

The fact of the matter is that the gospels are not -- and do not pretend to be -- objective reportage. They are the writings of religious activists with a message to deliver and a story to tell. If we as Christians would make this clear to our students, and if we could sensitize them to the offense given to Jews by the perpetuation of this New Testament view of the Pharisees, we shall have taken a giant step toward better interreligious relations.

PHARISEES: PROBLEMS AND POSSIBILITIES

(A Joint Perspective)

Problems

1. Many Christians hold a doctrine of literal biblical inspiration that does not allow any questioning of the historical truth and reliability of the gospels' presentation of the Pharisees. Yet to condemn the Pharisees for being the legalists that the gospels represent them to be, and at the same time to understand the Pharisees to be representative of the Jewish people, is to espouse anti-Semitism.

2. Some Jews refuse to go beyond labeling the New Testament anti-Semitic. This is not simply anachronistic; it is simplistic, inflammatory and unnecessary.

Possibilities

1. Jewish children studying the Pharisees would do well to analyze some of the images and arguments of the apostle Paul, whose writings abound in examples of Pharisaic haggadic midrash.

2. Christian students will profit from exposure to Jewish literature about the Pharisees and some of the famous teachers such as Hillel and Shammai. They will in this way get a fuller picture of these heroes of Judaism and of the diversity and vitality of Jewish thought in New Testament times.

ISRAEL

(A Jewish Perspective)

When the First Temple was destroyed and the Jews led into Exile more than 2500 years ago, the Psalmist wrote: "By the waters of Babylon, there we sat down, yea, we wept...If I forget thee, O Jerusalem, let my right hand forget her cunning. Let my tongue cleave to the roof of my mouth if I remember thee not, if I set not Jerusalem above my chiefest joy." Historically, even by the sixth century B.C.E., the survival of both Judaism as a religion and the Jews as a people had already been inextricably linked to the land of Israel for centuries.

Almost the entire Hebrew Scriptures is one long story of God's promise of the land to Abraham and all his descendants (Genesis 17), and of how the Jewish people gained it, lost it and regained it.

From the time of the Exodus, about 1300 B.C.E., Jews have lived in that land continuously. Not all went into exile at the fall of the First Temple in 586 B.C.E. Even after the Romans destroyed the Second Temple in 70 C.E., and the Jews went into exile once more, close to one and a half million Jews remained in the land. Indeed, until the fifth century B.C.E., most of the inhabitants of the land were Jews.

Throughout the Diaspora, in all the centuries of their wandering, the Jews refused to give up hope of a return to this land where they could live once more under the sovereignty of God. Every day, for almost 2000 years, pious Jews have prayed for the restoration of the land. Every holiday celebration contains reminders of the pilgrimages to the Temple in Jerusalem. Services for the Day of Atonement and the Seder ceremony during Passover end with the affirmation, "Next year in Jerusalem." The cry of Russian Jews to this day is, "Next year in Jerusalem." For the last 1900 years Jews have constantly spoken of, prayed for, never stopped yearning for the land, for Eretz Yisrael.

By the late nineteenth century, the rise of anti-Semitism, exemplified by the Dreyfus case in France (1894) and the Tsarist pogroms in Russia, convinced the Jews that a return to the Holy Land was necessary, not just for the spiritual survival of Judaism, but for the very physical survival of the Jewish people. More than anyone else, it was Theodor Herzl who served as a catalyst to bring religious and political Zionists together and who thus made a return to the land more than a dream. Early pioneers emigrated to Palestine where they bought desert land, worked the soil, and made barren land bloom again. By independence in 1948 these chalutzim (pioneers) had reclaimed 250,000 acres of land and planted five million trees.

The modern State of Israel was created by the United Nations General Assembly in 1947 after the Holocaust, which had resulted in the death of six million Jews, and after the refusal of western society to accept the thousands of Jewish refugees who survived. The United Nations divided Palestine into two lands: one Arab, one Jewish. The new land of Israel accepted the partition plan, but the Arabs have not done so to this day. When independence was declared in 1948, five Arab nations attacked Israel. The Israelis fought for and won their independence, and all the land that is now part of Israel was obtained either by purchase or as a result of subsequent wars initiated against Israel.

Holidays, whether ancient pilgrimage festivals such as Sukkot, Pesach and Shavuot, or modern ones such as Israel Independence Day, have their origins in the land of Israel, and religious school celebrations stress this ancient attachment to the land. Since Hebrew is the official language of Israel, as well as the language of prayer in Judaism, it is taught on both levels in the classroom. Feelings about Israel are also transmitted through song.

Ever since its creation in modern days, Israel has been a source of spiritual strength and renewal, a place where Jews could live as part of a majority culture, a physical haven for all persecuted Jews, and a land whose existence is essential for their continued survival.

ISRAEL

(A Christian Perspective)

Among Christians, "Israel" has three meanings. The first is a sacred and non-political meaning: Israel is the name of God's chosen people, the descendants of Jacob (whose name was itself changed to Israel), the people of the Old Covenant, the people that God through Moses brought out of Egypt and into the promised land. Later on, "Israel" is understood to include the people of the New Covenant, the Christian Church, the "New Israel." In this usage, Israel is the Church's traditional term for God's chosen and faithful people. Neither Jewish ethnic peoplehood nor the modern State of Israel has anything to do with this first understanding of "Israel."

The second meaning is secular and political. It refers to the modern State of Israel. This second usage is in no sense related to the first. The State of Israel is simply a modern Near Eastern state. The State has biblical referents, of course, but these are not the ground on which Israel's legitimacy is assumed or argued. This is why, when some Christian groups voice support for the State of Israel, they speak in terms of "fair play" or "the eradication of anti-Semitism," and not in terms of "destiny" or "a homeland for the Jewish people."

The third meaning of Israel is sacred _and_ political. Israel is both the historical Jewish people and the modern State of Israel. Christian groups that understand Israel in this way usually base their support for modern Israel on biblical prophecies. They see the establishment of the State of Israel as a necessary event in these "last days" before the "end of all things" and the Second Coming of Christ.

All three of these understandings of Israel may be seen in Christian churches today. Israel and its successor, the "New Israel," the people of God, is still a significant thread in the teaching of the Orthodox churches (and also, until recent times, in the ecclesiology of the Roman Catholic Church). Israel is the modern political state without special theological arguments for its support, according to much main line, liberal Protestant thinking. The _re_-establishment of the State of Israel in modern times is, according to conservative Protestant bodies and sects, the beginning of the end in God's plan. The recent rapid growth of fundamentalist Protestantism in the United States has multiplied proponents of this sacred-political view of Israel. Although some Jews welcome this surge of support for Israel, many Jews and Christians are alarmed at the possible consequences of considering the modern state as a transitory element in a theological scenario for the end of the world.

ISRAEL: PROBLEMS AND POSSIBILITIES

(A Joint Perspective)

Problems

1. The problems of modern Israel hold no more importance for many Christians than the problems of France. There is no uniquely Christian interest in the State of Israel among many Christians. Therefore, Christian actions in behalf of the Jewish people in general and Israel in particular fall under the category of social action and not interreligious affairs.

2. Israel is not mentioned in many Christian religious education programs except as an ancient biblical land. It is not surprising, then, that most Christian laity know little about the Zionist movement, the Balfour Declaration or the role of the Holocaust as factors in the establishment of the modern State of Israel.

3. Christians by and large are not sensitive to the fact that, for most Jews, the people and the land of Israel are inseparable, and that the theology of the people of God expressed in Scripture includes a native land.

4. Jews are unaware that Christians lack knowledge of how the State of Israel came to be. As a result, Jews all too often mistakenly assume that lack of enthusiastic Christian support for their concerns about Israel is a manifestation of anti-Semitism.

5. Christian and Jewish support for Israel's right to exist is sometimes misinterpreted as support for particular Israeli government policies.

Possibilities

1. Christian high school level teachers could stress the continuity of the land of Israel from biblical times to the present by tracing its political history since those biblical times.

2. Christian teachers might trace the biblical theology of the land as expressed throughout Hebrew Scriptures, and especially in Deuteronomy.

3. Christian teachers in primary grades could make reference to Israel as a place which still exists when they tell Bible stories. They could cease calling the country "Palestine" (which has no biblical basis anyway) and certainly refer to it less often as "the Holy Land."

4. Teachers at the secondary level could study the Holocaust as more than an atrocity. The meaning of the experience for the Jewish people and for humankind could be studied via any one of several good and currently available texts.

5. The culture and language of modern Israel could be introduced to Christian students in the intermediate grades through recordings, folk dances and church/synagogue exchanges. The linguistic continuity of idiom and imagery could be used to demonstrate the historical attachment of people, land and culture.

6. Students and adults of both faiths should be taught about Christian resolutions in support of Israel.

7. Jewish teachers could trace the history of the Christian theological term "Israel" as it is used in the New Testament to denote "the people of God" -- old and new.

January 1982

Experimental
Educational
Editions

JEWS and CHRISTIANS:

teaching about each other

A MANUAL FOR TEACHERS

Part 3: Guidelines and Conclusion

A Joint Project of

The Department of Interreligious Affairs
Union of American Hebrew Congregations

The Commission on Christian-Jewish Relations
Episcopal Diocese of Long Island

1981

edited by
Lawrence McCoombe
and Annette Daum

UNION of AMERICAN HEBREW CONGREGATIONS
NEW YORK

MISSION AND MITZVOT

(A Jewish Perspective)

The mission of the Jewish people is to "be a light unto the nations" (Isaiah). Judaism does not seek converts as part of its mission, and has not done so since the early centuries of the Common Era.

Jews are to bring the knowledge of the one God and the moral code of Judaism to the world by leading lives based on the performance of mitzvot, those commandments which stem from the teachings of the Torah. Some of the most important passages are found in the Mosaic Code (Exodus), in the Holiness Code (Leviticus, particularly Chapter 19), and the Deuteronomic Code of Laws. Traditional Jews count 613 commandments in all and stress observance of ritual and such personal mitzvot as kashrut (dietary laws), and the wearing of tefillin; Reform Jews place greater emphasis on observance of those commands for justice which affect society as a whole.

The performance of mitzvot is one of the greatest joys and privileges in Judaism. By their deeds, Jews show their love of God and all humanity. The Jewish people are to act as co-partners with God in the creation of a better world, so that all people may come to live together in peace in a society based on justice, mercy, compassion and righteousness.

The Bar/Bat Mitzvah (literally son/daughter of the commandment) ceremony, which takes place at the age of thirteen, symbolizes that the student, after a number of years of preparation, is now old enough and knowledge-able enough to assume his/her responsibilities as a Jew: to lead services, to be part of the minyan, and perform other mitzvot that make the student a good person and a good Jew. While Orthodox, Conservative and Reform Jews may differ in the way they perform mitzvot, what is important is that all will say the same prayer, Sh'ma, to the same God with the same feeling; that all will be performing mitzvot to help Jews and other people in need.

Knowledge and understanding of Torah necessarily precedes the performance of mitzvot. Students should discuss how to apply the commandments today and be encouraged to develop class mitzvah projects, such as protesting the treatment of Soviet Jews and/or helping patients in a local nursing home.

Throughout their education, students are taught that performance of mitzvot is more important than adherence to a set of beliefs, that mitzvot are acts of tzedakah, of justice and righteousness, that are re-quired of the Jews as a community.

MISSION AND MITZVOT

(A Christian Perspective)

The Church exists by mission as fire does by burning. "Being sent" is an essential aspect of the Church's life. Hence, where there are Christians, there will be mission. On this much all Christians agree. But the precise shape, thrust and mode of that mission will vary from denomination to denomination, from congregation to congregation, even from Christian to Christian.

For some, mission means verbal and overt evangelism. For others, it means ministering to the needs of a suffering world. For still others, mission means living in the world in a manner which allows others to see one's life as shaped and fulfilled in the following of the Christian way. And, finally, for some, mission means coping with reality as one encounters it in day-to-day living, attempting to discover and respond to God's ongoing redemptive action.

These modes of mission overlap and are interrelated, and seldom does any Christian or any church opt for a single form of mission to the total exclusion of the others. Still, both Christians and Jews should be aware that such a variety of emphases does exist.

It is imperative that both Jewish and Christian teachers bear constantly in mind that whatever they teach about Christian mission, they present only a partial picture of that mission.

Statements beginning with "Christians believe" ought to be looked at very carefully and perhaps altered to read "some Christians believe," or "we believe," and sometimes even "I believe." We must convey to the children that, whatever Christian mission may be, it has no monolithic and universally agreed upon mode of expression.

MISSION AND MITZVOT: PROBLEMS AND POSSIBILITIES

(A Joint Perspective)

Problems

1. Christian texts often misunderstand "law" and "commandment" and portray them as limiting, restrictive, essentially negative elements.

2. Jewish teachers do not always realize that a heavy emphasis is placed on social action as part of the mission of some Christian denominations, but instead present all of Christianity as being interested only in the world to come. This reflects a failure to perceive the diversity of Christian viewpoints.

3. Christians fail to realize that Jews regard attempts at conversion as a lack of respect for their religious beliefs. They do not understand that Jewish concern in this context is realistically rooted in centuries of coerced conversions and of suffering for the sake of Jewish integrity.

4. Jews often interpret Christian mission to mean that all Christian denominations actively seek to convert Jews. This is simply not the case.

5. Certain mitzvot which were part of the living Jewish tradition received by Jesus (e.g., "Love the Lord your God with all your heart, and with all your soul, and with all your mind, and with all your strength"; "Love your neighbor as yourself") are credited by some Christian teachers and texts to Jesus alone, without recognition of their centrality to the ethos of Judaism, then and now. The implication left with the student is that all that is good began with Jesus.

6. Most Jews are unaware that Judaism in the beginning of the Common Era was a heavily proselytizing religion. Most Christians, on the other hand, do not understand why modern Judaism is no longer a proselytizing religion.

7. Jews tend to see mission as elective and non-essential. Christians see mission as essential to the identity of the Church.

Possibilities

1. "Love your neighbor as yourself." How do we show our love of neighbor? Can we develop joint social action projects to do this?

2. Since both Christians and Jews today are threatened by aggressive and unethical proselytizing methods used by various cult and missionary groups, we could work together to establish guidelines for ethics in faith communication.

CHOSENNESS AND COVENANT

(A Jewish Perspective)

"If you will hearken unto My voice, and keep My commandments, then ye shall be Mine own treasure from among all peoples...and ye shall be a kingdom of priests and a holy people." (Exodus 19:5)

Jews have always understood the concept of chosenness as indicative of their greater responsibility and obligation to fulfill God's commandments; as election for special duties, rather than special privileges.

While some Jews would consider that God chose the Israelites, others would consider that the Israelites chose God. What is important is that the Jews were the first people to adopt a belief in one God, to accept the teachings of Torah; and that for thousands of years Jews have believed that they are in a covenantal relationship with God which began with God's promise to Noah and was extended through Abraham, the Patriarchs, Moses, and the Prophets. The Israelites were chosen for a special purpose, to be the bearers of God's ethical covenant and to bring the knowledge of that covenant and of the one God to all humanity.

Judaism's covenant responsibilities are demanding and explicit. As described in Exodus, Leviticus, and Deuteronomy, the Israelites are to be a holy people. They are, for example, to keep the Sabbath, to refrain from idolatry, to leave the corners of the fields and the gleanings of the vineyard for the poor and the stranger. They are not to place a stumbling block before the blind nor curse the deaf. Above all, they must obey the command to "Love thy neighbor as thyself."

The brit at Sinai indicates that this pact was made with the people Israel as a community. Jews are born into this covenantal relationship. As a people they are to fulfill their promise to obey God's commandments and God promises to cherish them, care for them, protect them, and lead them to a land flowing with milk and honey.

This covenant with Judaism was established long before Jesus; it continues to the present day and beyond. The Jewish people are now and forever the servants of God, and they have an eternal mandate to bring universal ethical monotheism to all peoples on earth.

While the brit at Sinai indicates that the Jews have a special responsibility to carry out all the precepts of the Torah, the rabbis of talmudic times describe seven universal laws based on an interpretation of the Noachide Covenant (Genesis 9:4-15), which are incumbent upon all human beings:

> Establishment of courts of justice
> Prohibition of blasphemy, idolatry, adultery, bloodshed, robbery
> Prohibition of eating flesh cut from a living animal
> (Sanhedrin 56A. Compare Acts 15:19-20)

People who observe these laws are considered to be "pious of the Gentiles," and assured of a portion in the world to come.

God's love, then, is not reserved exclusively for Israelites. As the prophet Amos taught, "Are ye not as the children of the Ethiopian unto me, O children of Israel? saith the Lord. Have I not brought up Israel out of the land of Egypt, and the Philistine from Caphtor, and Aram from Kir?" (Amos 9:7).

CHOSENNESS AND COVENANT

(A Christian Perspective)

Christians speak of God's covenant with the Children of Israel as the sacral event by which Israel was chosen to be God's people in return for their allegiance, worship and obedience. "Covenant" here is a once-for-all event, sealed with the blood of sacrifice.

The imagery of sacrifice and once-for-all-ness has encouraged traditionally-oriented Christians to see the covenant of God with Israel as a "type" or model (of inferior importance, for that is the way with types and models) the New Covenant in Christ.

There is a great difference of outlook within Christianity when it comes to deciding whether God's New Covenant in Christ nullifies the Old Covenant with the Jewish people. Traditionalist Christians say that the New Covenant renders the old one void and that any Jew who wishes to be in a covenant relationship with God must become a part of God's New Israel, the Church. Fewer in number and at the other end of the spectrum are those Christians who believe that the Christian covenant is other than -- but not superior to -- the Old Covenant. These are people who believe God still chooses Israel and has established this New Covenant to include Gentiles, although anyone may enter into it by baptism. (This view is a minority one among Christian laity, although the apostle Paul may have been its earliest proponent.)

CHOSENNESS AND COVENANT: PROBLEMS AND POSSIBILITIES

(A Joint Perspective)

Problems

1. Christians sometimes feel shortchanged by the Jewish viewpoint on this subject. This occurs when the Jew affirms the covenant of God with the Jewish people and asks the Christian to join in affirming the continuing validity of that covenant, but reserves judgment on whether Christians also have a valid covenantal relationship with God (beyond the Noachian Covenant).

2. Whereas Jews give emphasis to the social responsibilities incurred by virtue of chosenness, Christians place the emphasis on God's historical choice of the Hebrew people as a "saving event" in a salvation history whose culmination is in the death/resurrection of Jesus.

3. Christians misunderstand the Jewish self-perception about being "chosen," assuming that Jews think themselves somehow superior to Gentiles.

4. When Jews or Christians lay claim to be the only people of God, such an action constitutes a judgment on the other.

Possibilities

1. High school level students might explore the various ancient Near Eastern covenants outside the Bible to discover what the word "covenant" means outside the Hebrew Scriptures. The several biblical covenants could then be compared with these.

2. Interfaith adult education about the Bible would, as always, be helpful in exploring our self-perceptions as covenanted/chosen people.

3. Joint exploration of non-exclusive approaches to our respective covenant relationships might prove fruitful in building mutual respect and affirmation. Can only one covenant exist? Why not two? Why not one covenant with two modes of expression?

PRAYER

(A Jewish Perspective)

In Judaism, prayer is considered the service of the heart; it is a way of communicating with God, and is approached with all our heart, all our soul and all our might.

There are many ways of reaching out to God. In ancient days, Jews communicated with God by offering sacrifices which were accompanied by rituals and ceremonies. Eventually these ceremonies became so complicated that only special religious leaders (Temple priests and Levites) could conduct them or lead the singing.

Religious practices began to change after the destruction of the First Temple in 586 B.C.E. Without a temple, the priests could no longer offer sacrifices; therefore, a new form of worship was required. In exile, in Babylonia the Jewish people began to gather on the Sabbath to study the Holy Book, and to reach out to God directly, with words, without priests, altars or sacrifices.

The custom of coming together to study and pray in a neighborhood synagogue continued even after the Jews returned to their land, even though the Temple at Jerusalem was rebuilt. It was the existence of the synagogue that enabled Judaism to survive. After the fall of the Second Temple, Jews were able to continue to worship the one God, using prayer as a substitute for sacrifice. The design of the synagogue service as developed at that time was incorporated into early Christian worship. The first part of the Eucharistic Service retains the structure of Jewish worship services at the beginning of the Common Era.

Prayer consists of more than mere words and can take different forms. Traditionally, in Judaism, study of Torah is regarded as prayer and acts of kindness (gemilut chasadim) are also considered a form of prayer.

The heart of the worship service for all branches of Judaism is the Sh'ma, the watchword of the faith, which proclaims that there is one God for all humanity who exists for all eternity. Ultimately, students learn that prayer, whether expressed in terms of praise, petition or thanks to God, inspires us to remember the commandments; to do justice, to love mercy and to understand God's will.

"May it by Thy will, O God, to extend peace, great and wondrous, in the universe. Let all the peoples of the earth recognize and know the innermost truth; that we are not come into this world for quarrel and division, nor for hate and jealousy, contrariness and bloodshed; but we are come into this world to recognize and know Thee. Be Thou blessed forever." (Chasidic literature)

PRAYER

(A Christian Perspective)

Prayer is, for both Christians and Jews, humanity's godward conscious-
ness, arising out of experience and given expression in word or deed.
At its heart, prayer is not a simple petitioning of the Creator for
various favors, but a celebration of God as a presence recognized in
and through the human experience. This recognition has been verbal-
ized in many ways. Some of these verbalizations have proven to be more
adeqately expressive of the "God-experience" than others. These are
the prayers which have lasted, and which have been transmitted to us
in the form of "traditional" prayers.

Further, God deals with persons not only individually, but in groups,
in communities. Hence, there are corporate prayers, expressions toward
God by the believing community, celebrating that particular community's
special experience of God. These corporate prayers are the backbone
of liturgical prayer, both Christian and Jewish.

PRAYER: PROBLEMS AND POSSIBILITIES

(A Joint Perspective)

Problems

1. Christian and Jewish educators alike have problems with the relevance of prayer for many of their students.

2. Many Christian clergy deliver public invocations which assume that Christian doctrine and language are acceptable to the audience or congregation. This reflects a lack of sensitivity and should not be done.

3. Christians should realize that, while they may recite Jewish prayers without compromising their faith, Jews cannot join in prayers that pay homage to Jesus as God or the Son of God. Further, the Lord's Prayer, although its words do not pay such homage, cannot be used by Jews because it has become as much a symbol of Christianity as the cross.

4. When Jews teach the origin of prayers like the _Alenu_ and the _Kol Nidre_, which were altered or added as a result of Christian misunderstanding or persecution, they should indicate that this was the result of an _ancient_ problem and is not to be taken as reflection of contemporary attitudes.

Possibilities

1. Exchange traditional prayers and prayerbooks. Explore how someone else prays by attending services at each other's houses of worship.

2. Christians should acknowledge the origin of those rituals, customs and prayers that stem from Jewish sources, and vice versa.

3. Christian students can memorize and use Jewish prayers. To a degree, this constitutes walking in the other person's shoes, which cannot but increase sympathetic interreligious understanding.

4. Jews and Christians should be aware that certain prayers that are offensive to Jews have been deleted from Christian prayerbooks in recent years because they no longer reflect sound Christian theology.

5. Hold an interfaith dialogue on worship to include information on all of the above.

INTERMARRIAGE

(A Jewish Perspective)

The traditional prohibition against intermarriage in biblical days was religious in nature, and served as protection against idolatry. Were pagan practices in surrounding cultures to be introduced into the family, they would undermine such fundamental precepts of Judaism as the worship of the one God.

While the dangers of intermarriage are expressed by Abraham and Rebekah in Genesis, by Moses in Deuteronomy, and by Joshua, the strongest statement occurs in the Book of Ezra.

After the Babylonian Exile, when Ezra the Scribe led the Jewish people back to rebuild Palestine, he was shocked to find so many of his people married to people who practiced pagan rites. When he heard this, he tore his garments and his beard, and made the men take an oath that they would divorce their foreign wives so that they could practice the faith of Torah. Intermarriage was forbidden then so that both the land and the faith could be restored.

Biblical scholars generally agree that the Book of Ruth was written as a protest against Ezra's harsh policies, and was included in Hebrew Scriptures as evidence that these policies were not universally accepted. In this book, Ruth, a Moabite, shows her loyalty to her mother-in-law Naomi, to the Jewish people, and to the one God of Judaism, in the following passage:

> Entreat me not to leave thee
> And to return from following after thee;
> For whither thou goest, I will go;
> And whither thou diest I will die;
> Thy people shall be my people,
> And thy God, my God.

To emphasize Ruth's importance, the end of the book describes how the great King David, from whom the Messiah is expected to come, was descended from Ruth.

This tension between advocates of strict policies against intermarriage and those who support accommodation is still evident in modern times. Especially since the Holocaust, intermarriage is seen by many as a betrayal of the millions of Jews who suffered and died for their faith, and as a threat to the very survival of both Judaism and the Jewish people. For this reason, all branches of Judaism oppose intermarriage and most rabbis refuse to officiate such marriages.

Since intermarriage is bound to exist in an open society and appears to be an increasing problem, a few rabbis will participate in such wedding ceremonies in the hope of encouraging the Jewish partner to maintain his/her relationship with the Jewish community. Another sign of flexibility is the growing acceptance of such families into Reform and Conservative synagogues despite the lack of any formal conversion on the part of the non-Jewish partner.

Perhaps the most volatile, emotional and divisive problem facing such couples is the question of their children's religion. Courses in the upper grades of the religious school explore these problems and the emotional consequence of making decisions which may result in the severing of ties to the family, the people and the faith.

INTERMARRIAGE

(A Christian Perspective)

The maintenance of Jewish peoplehood is not a strong element in traditional Christian theology. The continuing existence of the Jewish people, in fact, raises embarrassing questions for those Christians who see the Church as the New Israel, replacing the Jews as the people whom God has chosen. It is not surprising, therefore, that the Church has traditionally had, at best, no special interest in whether a Jew marries a non-Jew -- unless, of course, the non-Jew is a Christian. But then the issue is not that of intermarriage of Jews with others. It is the issue of Christians marrying non-Christians.

The degree of Christian concern about marriage outside the faith varies among denominations (the more conservative churches being the more adamant in opposing such unions), among congregations within the same denomination, and even among families within a single congregation, depending on the degree of their religious commitment and involvement.

No Christian denomination encourages intermarriage, even between members of two Christian denominations. The reluctance of Christian clergy to endorse such relationships is today grounded more in pastoral considerations about the effect of religious differences on the parties and on any children they may have then in theological considerations about the nature of Christian marriage or the rightness or wrongness of beliefs.

Ironically, it is the very persons who are considering marriage who often seem least concerned about their religious differences. They assign little importance to specific religious affiliation as a factor in marriage.

INTERMARRIAGE: PROBLEMS AND POSSIBILITIES

(A Joint Perspective)

Problems

1. Christians seem unaware of the importance of this issue for Jews.

2. When they explore with their own people the consequences of inter-marriage, Jews and Christians should not denigrate either religion or its adherents.

3. Problems are created for <u>both</u> partners when either one stipulates that the other must convert or "raise the children in my religion" as a condition of marriage.

4. Both Christian and Jewish young people fail to realize the role which their religious training and tradition have played in their own personality development and attitude formation. They cannot, therefore, easily assess the degree of adjustment required for a "successful" religiously mixed marriage.

Possibilities

1. Using the expertise of professional religious leaders of the com-munity, explore with teenage classes the teachings and practices of Christianity and Judaism with special focus on home and family life (celebrations, customs, special observances, rites of passage, etc.). The object here is to assist students in assessing the full implications of marriage for home and family life.

2. Reach out to students on the college campus to help them under-stand the consequences of a "divided family" and the possible effect of a "delayed reaction" when religion becomes increasingly important as people grow older.

ALENU - The beginning portion of the concluding prayers of a Jewish service. It is one of the oldest prayers, originally recited only on Rosh Hashanah and Yom Kippur. It was incorporated into Shabbat and other services in the fourteenth century C.E.

Referred to as the Adoration, the Alenu summarizes many ideas found in other portions of the service such as:

- God created the world and rules over all creation
- There is one God.
- Human beings and God are partners in bringing the knowledge of the one God and acceptance of the one God to all peoples in the world.

ANGLICAN COMMUNION - A term designating those churches in communion with and acknowledging the leadership of the See of Canterbury. The following churches comprise the Anglican Communion: The Church of England, Church of England in Australia, Episcopal Church of Brazil (Igreja Episcopal do Brasil), Church in the Province of Burma, Anglican Church of Canada, Church of the Province of Central Africa, Anglican Church in Ceylon, Holy Catholic Church in China (Chung Hua Sheng Kung Hui), Church in the Province of the Indian Ocean, Church of Ireland, Holy Catholic Church in Japan (Nippon Seikokai), Episcopal Church in Jerusalem and the Middle East, Church of the Province of Kenya, Province of Melanesia, Church of the Province of New Zealand, Episcopal Church in Scotland, Church of the Province of South Africa, Province of Sudan, Church in the Province of Tanzania, Church of Uganda, Rwanda, Burundi, and Boga-Zaire, Church in Wales, Church of the Province of West Africa, Church in the Province of the West Indies, the Protestant Episcopal Church in the United States of America (Episcopal Church), and others not yet designated as included in any province.

ANTI-SEMITISM - Discrimination or prejudice against Jews and Judaism; persecution of Jews; vilification of Judaism. Anti-Semitism can take many forms, ranging from social, economic and physical isolation of Jews to a denial of civil and religious liberties, leading as it has to pogroms or the Holocaust.

APOSTLE - (Hebrew shaliach, Greek apostolos, both meaning "sent"). Originally a secular term denoting one's personal representative or agent empowered to act on one's behalf.

In Christian circles, the term came early to apply to the twelve chief disciples of Jesus whom he "sent out" with a mission. The original apostles are believed to have preached widely and to have organized Christian communities in various places. The resident leadership of

these congregations was then entrusted by the founding apostles to over-
seers (Greek <u>episkopoi</u>, English <u>bishops</u>) and elders (Greek <u>presbyteroi</u>).
Hence, the bishops are termed "successors of the apostles" inasmuch as
(a) they were set apart for this work by the apostles; and (b) their
task is to continue the apostolic ministry.

In the early Church, however, many more than twelve men called themselves "apostles." They wandered the countryside prophesying, preaching and visiting the churches in a sort of freelance charismatic
ministry.

In its broad usage, "apostle" denotes a missionary sent into an area
for the first time: e.g., Patrick, Apostle to Ireland.

<u>ASHKENAZI</u> - A Hebrew term originally applied to those Jews living in
Germany and Northern France. The term, as applied in modern times, also
includes Jews from Poland, Russia, the Scandinavian countries, as well
as their descendants and is used to distinguish them from those Jews
of Spanish or Mediterranean descent. (See Sephardim.)

Both groups have different rituals, social customs, music and language.
Yiddish, a language used by many Ashkenazi Jews, a mixture of German,
Russian, Polish and Hebrew, is familiar to many Americans.

The majority of American Jews are descended from an Ashkenazic tradition.

<u>BABYLONIAN EXILE</u> - The first exile of the Jewish people from their
homeland by the Babylonian King Nebuchadnezzar which took place in 586
B.C.E. The loss of the land and the destruction of the First Temple
had a profound effect upon the Jews and Judaism. As a result of this
experience, the Jews formed a strong attachment to the land, developed
new methods of worship and brought the concept of universal, ethical
monotheism to the world.

<u>CANON</u> - A term used to refer to those books which were formally approved
and officially accepted as sacred writings to be included in the Bible.
The Jewish Bible contains Hebrew Scriptures only; Christians add the New
Testament as well. Some Christian traditions include the Apocrypha.

<u>CHRISTMAS</u> - The Christian feast celebrating the Incarnation of God the
Son in the person of Jesus of Nazareth. Christmas was not a generally
observed feast in the Church until sometime in the fourth century. At
that time, the practice of the Church of Rome, which celebrated the
birth of Jesus on December 25, was widely adopted. The date for the
celebration was probably chosen because of its proximity to the feast
of the <u>Natalis Solis Invicti</u>. The festive mood of this pagan holiday
has remained an integral part of popular Christian observances.

For Christians, Christmas is not principally the celebration of the birthday of Jesus, but of the event by which God became man. The occasion, then, presents one of the central mysteries of the Christian faith. As such, Christmas is an essentially Christian holiday, not a universal one.

CHURCH - (Latin <u>ecclesia</u>). The word has two basic meanings: (1) a building set apart for Christian worship; (2) the people of God. (When used in this sense, the word is always spelled with a capital C.) Theologically, the Church is termed "the body of Christ," the continuing Incarnation, the "bride of Christ," and the people of God "called out" (the literal meaning of <u>ecclesia</u>) of the world.

CONVERSION - A change from adherence to one religious belief to adherence of another religious faith. For Judaism, conversion is a process involving a long period of thought and study which is deliberately undertaken. While there have been periods in Jewish history when Jews actively sought converts, it has never been a typical practice of the Jewish community. In Christian understanding, conversion is the result through a single experience focused on establishing a personal relationship with Jesus Christ.

DEICIDE - The charge that the Jewish people were/are responsible for the death of the Son of God.

DIASPORA - A Greek word meaning "scattering" which refers to the dispersion of the Jewish people outside of Palestine, beginning, historically, with the conquest of Palestine by the Romans.

DREYFUS CASE - In 1894, Alfred Dreyfus, a Jewish artillery captain attached to the general staff of the French Army, was falsely accused of selling military secrets to Germany.

Despite his innocence, Dreyfus was tried and convicted by a military court and sentenced to life imprisonment on Devil's Island. The case became a cause celebre. French novelists like Emile Zola and Anatole France and statesmen like George Clemenceau demanded justice and equality before the law. Evidence was uncovered linking Walsin Esterhazy, another officer, to the crime. Despite his guilt, he was tried by a military court and acquitted.

Public opinion was aroused and the military were forced to reopen the case. After only one hour of deliberation, Dreyfus was found guilty again, but his sentence was reduced to ten years. The repressive atmosphere was so great that Zola, himself, was imprisoned, eventually escaping to London. The Dreyfus case then became an explosive national issue. Continuous efforts to vindicate Dreyfus finally resulted in his exoneration by a civil supreme court in 1906. The proceedings, which were accompanied by outbreaks of anti-Semitism, had a profound effect upon Theodor Herzl who was, at that time, a foreign correspondent covering the case. Not long after, he became the founder of modern political Zionism, which he viewed as the only solution to anti-Semitism.

EASTER - The feast of the Resurrection of Jesus Christ and, hence, the most important Christian festival. The word "easter" itself is probably derived from the name of the Anglo-Saxon spring goddess "Eostre," whose feast was replaced by this celebration of the Resurrection.

In Asia Minor the early Christians celebrated the Passion/Resurrection of Jesus on the 14th day of the Jewish lunar month of Nisan. This was the day on which the Passover lambs were slaughtered. No matter on what day of the week Nisan 14 fell, these Asia Minor Christians celebrated what we would call "Easter" on that date. They became known as "Puartodecimans" ("fourteenthers").

The practice of the Church at Rome, however, was to celebrate the feast of the Resurrection on the Sunday following Nisan 14. The Council of Nicaea in 325 A.D. confirmed Roman usage by decreeing that Easter was to be observed on the Sunday following the full moon occurring on or after the vernal equinox (March 21). The theme and imagery of Passover have remained, however, and Easter is often termed "the Christian Passover."

HANUKKAH - The word means "dedication" and the holiday celebrates the rededication of the Temple to Jewish worship after the victory of the Maccabees in the first recorded fight for religious liberty which occurred in 165 B.C.E.

The Maccabees did not go to war to gain political freedom, although they obtained it as a result of their battle. They accepted the rule of Antiochus IV as long as they had religious freedom and only went to war when the King ordered all people, including the Jews, to worship the Greek god Zeus, placed an idol of Zeus in the Temple, and forbade the practice of all Jewish religious rites such as circumcision, the teaching of Torah and observance of the Sabbath.

The holiday is celebrated on the 25th day of Kislev in the Jewish calendar. Although the date can appear on the American calendar anywhere from late November to late December, there is no connection with Christmas. That date is not the date of a great battle or the day the Maccabees reconquered Jerusalem, but rather on the day the Temple was cleansed of idol worship and rededicated to Jewish worship.

The most important symbol of the holiday is the Menorah which is lit in a home-ceremony every night for the eight days of the holiday. Many legends have developed to explain these customs. A legend in the Talmud describes how one day's supply of holy oil for the Menorah lasted for eight days. Another says that soldiers, finding eight iron rods stuck in the walls, used them for a Menorah and placed candles in them. No one can speak with certainty about the historical reasons for the customs. Hanukkah is an important, though minor, holiday in Judaism because of its spiritual significance, because of its focus on Judaism's dedication to the worship of one God.

HILLEL - A revered rabbi and leader of the Pharisees who lived during the last half of the first century B.C.E. and the beginning of the first century C.E. A distinguished scholar, he established his own academy of learning which became famous for its liberal interpretation of Torah. Because of his brilliance, he was appointed President of the Sanhedrin (Jewish High Court). He was known for his humanity and many famous sayings are attributed to him, such as "Judge not your neighbor until you have come into his place," and "Do not do unto others as you would not have them do unto you."

HOLOCAUST - The dictionary definition is burnt offering; a great or total destruction of life, especially by fire.

For Jews, the Holocaust is the most shattering experience of modern history. The term is used in reference to the deliberate, planned annihilation of all Jews which took place under Nazi domination of Europe during World War II. This program of mass genocide resulted in the death of six million Jews, one third of the entire Jewish population of the world. It was a unique, traumatic event, without parallel in human history, and is viewed by many Jews as the culmination of centuries of Christian anti-Semitism; as the central event that will affect the relationship between Jews and Christians for generations to come.

JABNEH (YAVNEH) - A small town near the Mediterranean Sea to which Rabbi Johanan ben Zakkai and his followers escaped just before the fall of the Second Temple by the Romans. There he and his disciples established an academy which kept Jewish learning and Torah from being destroyed. Eventually, Jabneh became the center for Palestinian Judaism and a new Sanhedrin was established there.

KOL NIDRE - A famous prayer associated with the Day of Atonement, sung on the eve of Yom Kippur. This prayer, meaning literally, "all vows," has been the source of a great deal of misunderstanding between Jews and Christians in the past.

While its origin is uncertain, many scholars believe that the prayer was introduced by the Jews of Spain about 600 C.E. as a prayer-formula to seek release from vows made when many were forced to convert to Christianity by the West Goths. When they were free to return to Judaism, the Kol Nidre made it possible for them to be released from these vows made under duress.

In later years, Christians who did not know the background of this prayer, distrusted the Jews because they mistakenly thought this prayer made it possible for Jews to abrogate all vows, including contracts. Kol Nidre only releases Jews from unfulfilled promises made to God. It does not apply to promises or vows made between human beings. A Jew who wrongs another person must make atonement with -- and seek forgiveness from -- that person.

LAW - In Judaism. Jewish Law encompasses more than mere legal principles, for it means instruction, or teaching, and serves as a guide to enhance the quality of life.

Jewish Law (or Halachah*) is divided into two parts: (a) the Written Law is found in the Torah and includes ethical, family and ritual matters as well as civil and criminal codes; (b) the Oral Law includes all interpretations of the Written Law as well as the decisions and opinions of the rabbis throughout the centuries. A number of Codes of Law developed over the ages. The Shulchan Aruch, compiled by Joseph Karo in the sixteenth century C.E., remains the authoritative code for traditional Jews to this day. Reform Jews regard the ethical codes as binding for all time, but ritual and other technical matters are viewed as a product of a particular society and subject to varying interpretation.

In Christianity. (Cf. "Torah") - As used by Christians, the sense of this term derives from the writings of the Apostle Paul. Paul used the term "Torah" to designate "The Law," given so that humanity might distinguish between right and wrong, good and evil. Since man is, by nature, unable (as well as unwilling) to meet the demands of the Law, the giving of the Law had the effect of revealing humanity's sinfulness. The Law, then, shows how life should be lived, but does not empower one to live that life.

MACCABEES - The Maccabees were founders of the Hasmonean dynasty which ruled Judea from 165 B.C.E. until the Romans conquered the land.

Mattathias and his sons were known as "the Maccabees" because of their successful revolt for religious liberty against the Greek-Syrian King of Judea. Their victory enabled the Jews to rededicate the Holy Temple to Jewish worship in 165 B.C.E., an event which is celebrated at Hanukkah.

The name Maccabee may stem from the Hebrew word for hammer, supposedly because of the "hammer blows" they dealt to the Selucid Armies, or it

---

*See Talmud for additional information.

may be a contraction of the first syllables of their battle cry -- "Who is like unto Thee, O Lord?"   מִי כָמוֹכָה בָּאֵלִים יי ‎   M - C - B - Y.

MASORETIC TEXT - The Masoretes were Jewish scholars who worked over the centuries to preserve and transmit the most accurate spelling and pronunciation of Hebrew Scriptures. One of the Masoretic versions of the biblical text, produced in the tenth century C.E., gained general acceptance and is the standard Hebrew biblical text in use today among both Jews and Christians.

MINYAN - The word "minyan," which means "the count" refers to the minimum number of ten male Jews above the age of 13 who are necessary to form an official congregation required by Jewish tradition for community worship.

Traditionally, women are not counted as part of a minyan, a custom still adhered to by Orthodox Jews. Women are counted as part of a minyan in some Conservative synagogues today. Reform Judaism does not require a minyan to initiate public worship.

MITZVAH - Hebrew term meaning "commandment." Mitzvot (plural) are religious and moral obligations (expressed in the teachings of the Torah) which Jews must observe. According to tradition, there are 248 positive and 365 negative commandments.

PASSION NARRATIVE - An account of the suffering and death of Jesus (collectively called "the Passion"). The New Testament passion narratives recount the events of the last two days of Jesus' life, including the Last Supper, the agony in Gethsemane, the arrest, trial(s), crucifixion, death and burial. Each of the four New Testament gospels includes a passion narrative: Matthew 26-27, Mark 15-14, Luke 22-23, John 13-19 (especially 18-19). These narratives, it is generally agreed, antedate the gospels in which they are found.

PATRIARCHS - Abraham, Isaac and Jacob were the rulers of their tribal families and are revered as the founders of the Hebrew people. Their wives, Sarah, Rebecca, Rachel and Leah are honored as the Matriarchs.

PENTECOST (literally "fiftieth") - For Christians this festival marks the empowerment of the early Church by the Holy Spirit (see Acts 2). The name of the feast is derived from the Greek word for the Jewish feast of Shavuot (q.v.).

PESACH - The Passover festival of the Jewish people which commemorates their redemption from bondage in Egypt.

POGROM - From the Russian meaning "riot" or "devastation." The organized massacres of Jewish communities which took place in the late nineteenth century and early twentieth century C.E., mostly under the Czarist regimes of Russia and Poland. These attacks were often provoked by government officials and resulted in the deaths of thousands of Jews and the destruction of many Jewish communities.

PROPHECY - Prophets, both male and female, existed among the Israelites even from ancient times. They were inspired people and their "prophecy" was not so much a prediction of the future as it was a religious and moral message from God. The prophecies were often messages against idolatry, injustice and immorality.

PROSELYTIZE - Actively to seek the conversion of people to the beliefs and tenets of one's own religious faith.

RABBINIC JUDAISM - That interpretation of Judaism which developed through oral and written interpretations of the Torah by the great rabbis of talmudic times, approximately 30 C.E. to 500 C.E.

REDEMPTION - Judaism views redemption in an historical sense. The central redemptive event in Judaism is the physical saving of the Israelites from slavery in Egypt. For Christians, the central event in Christianity is the redemption of humanity with the coming of Jesus as the Messiah.

RESURRECTION - In Judaism. Rising of the dead in bodily form. The earliest references to this concept in Judaism are found in the Books of Isaiah, Ezekiel and Daniel. The idea became important during the days of the Second Temple and was promoted by the Pharisees, who expected this to take place shortly with the coming of a Messiah and the end of days. There were differences of opinion concerning the concept of resurrection in Judaism, with some adhering to the belief that only the righteous would be resurrected, while others taught that all would be resurrected but the just would be rewarded and the wicked punished.

Orthodox Jews today still believe in the concept, but no longer expect the imminent coming of the end of days. Reform Judaism rejects the concept of bodily resurrection, advocating instead immortality of the soul, while Conservative Jews are not united on the subject.

In Christianity. Generally, resurrection denotes a rising from the dead. Christians use the term with a more precise meaning that has central and far-reaching implications.

> "The resurrection of Jesus Christ represents the watershed of New Testament history and the central point of its faith. On the historical plane it marks the division between the earthly life of Jesus and the apostolic

age; but it is seen also as nothing less than a new act of creation, signalizing the divide between the old world and the new, and inaugurating that resurrection order of life which is one day to be the only one. It has connections backward with the promise of resurrection already held out in the Old Testament and the Apocrypha, and forward with the general resurrection at the last day. But its center is that invisible point on the "third day," where faith and history meet in a relationship which remains as problematic as it is indissoluble."

(J.A.T. Robinson, "Resurrection in the New Testament," Interpreter's Dictionary of the Bible IV. Nashville: Abington Press, 1962, p. 43)

The Pharisees taught that in the messianic age there would be a bodily resurrection in which all the dead would be raised (with the exception of certain apostates). The Sadducees did not accept this teaching.

Today, Orthodox Jews continue in the expectation of a bodily resurrection "in the end of days" with the coming of the Messiah. Reform Judaism rejects this concept. Christians believe that in the resurrection of Jesus this hoped-for messianic age, the "new creation" has already begun. The end has broken into the midst. Christians become participants in this new creation at their baptism. Through this sacrament, Christians believe they share in Christ's death and resurrection. Being thus "in Christ" they are partakers of "new life" now as well as recipients of the promise of eternal life at the final resurrection.

Jesus' resurrection means, then, for Christians that the final event has already occurred; God's "last word" about human destiny has already been spoken. The new creation is already present in a mysterious and hidden way. It will become fully realized only at the last day.

SABBATH (Shabbat) - A holy day, to be observed as a day of rest, study, peace and joy. For Jews, the Sabbath begins at sundown on Friday evening and ends at sundown on Saturday evening. It is celebrated as a sign of the covenant between God and the Jewish people as well as in remembrance of God's creation and redemption.

SADDUCEES - Originally a Jewish religious priestly class which became also a political party in the time of the Second Temple. They were the aristocrats of their day. They believed in strict, literal adherence to the laws of Torah without allowing for interpretation. As members of the ruling class, they were politically influential and advocated greater assimilation with the Hellenists.

SANHEDRIN - When the Jews returned from the Babylonian Exile in the sixth century B.C.E., Ezra the Scribe convened a group of seventy scholars, called the Great Assembly, to help him interpret the laws of Torah. This Assembly was patterned after the seventy elders who helped Moses dispense justice. They were the predecessors of the Sanhedrin which was the highest Jewish court during the last part of the Second Commonwealth. It acted in the capacity of both a senate and a supreme court which discussed and decided, by vote, how to interpret the laws of Torah as they applied to the society of that day. Membership was open only to men chosen for their scholarship and intellectual ability.

The Great Sanhedrin had seventy-one members and met only in the Temple at Jerusalem. A smaller type of Sanhedrin, with twenty-three members, met both in Jerusalem and in the major districts of Palestine. Their power was severely limited when under foreign rule, such as under Roman domination at the beginning of the Common Era. Scholars disagree over whether the Sanhedrin could administer the death penalty or had power to act in political cases during the period of Jesus' life. Crimes against the state had to be brought before the Roman authorities.

There was a remarkable resemblance between the Jewish system of law as it developed under the leadership of the Sanhedrin and the modern American legal system. There was a presumption of innocence. The accused had the right to counsel, the right to call witnesses, and to confront accusers. In addition, all those accused could not be forced to testify against themselves and had the right to testify in their own behalf, as well as the right of appeal.

While the Jews were expected to abide by the majority opinion, those who disagreed had the right to issue a minority statement explaining the nature of the disagreement.

SEPHARDIM - A term originally applied to Jews of Spanish and Portugese descent. After their forced expulsion from Spain in the late fifteenth century, they dispersed to other lands such as Turkey, Syria, Palestine, North Africa, etc.

Some of these Jews fled to South America until, threatened once more by the Inquisition, they fled to New Amsterdam, thus becoming the first group of Jews to settle in North America in 1654.

Sephardim have their own rituals, customs, culture, music and language which differs from that of the Ashkenazim. Some use a language, Ladino, a mixture of Castilian Spanish and Hebrew. The Sephardic pronunciation of Hebrew is used in modern Israel.

SHAMMAI - A prominent teacher of the first century B.C.E., Shammai was a member of the Pharisees. He advocated strict adherence to the letter of the law and was a colleague and rival of the great teacher Hillel.

SHAVUOT - Hebrew for the Feast of Weeks, Shavuot was one of the three agricultural pilgrimage festivals of the year for the Israelites. This holiday is also known as Pentecost, because it begins on the fiftieth day after the second day of Pesach, upon completion of seven weeks of the counting of the Omer (the sheaf of the barley harvest).

Shavuot is traditionally regarded as the time when God gave the Ten Commandments on Mount Sinai. The Book of Ruth is read at synagogue services, both because of its reference to Jewish agricultural customs and because of Ruth's embracing Judaism.

SH'MA - The most important affirmation in Judaism:

> "Hear, O Israel: The Lord our God, the Lord is One.
> And thou shalt love the Lord thy God with all thy heart,
> and with all thy soul, and with all thy might. And
> these words which I command thee this day, shall be
> upon thy heart; and thou shalt teach them diligently
> unto thy children, and shalt talk of them when thou
> sittest in thy house, and when thou walkest by the way,
> and when thou liest down, and when thou risest up. And
> thou shalt bind them for a sign upon thy hand, and they
> shall be for frontlets between thine eyes. And thou
> shalt write them upon the door-posts of thy house, and
> upon thy gates. That ye may remember, and do all My
> commandments, and be holy unto your God. I am the Lord
> your God, who brought you out of the land of Egypt, to
> be your God: I am the Lord your God."

The words (Deut. 6:4-9, 11:13-21, Num. 5:37-41) serve as a reminder that God is one and unique and that all humanity are children of the one, eternal God.

SIN - In Judaism. In Judaism, sin is an act of commission, not a state of being. The Hebrew word for sin sued most often is "het" which means "missing the mark" as in shooting an arrow and missing the bull's eye. In Judaism, confession for sins committed against God are made directly to God without any intermediaries. The worst sin in Judaism is that which is committed against another person. Offenses against people can only be forgiven by the person who is wronged, after an act of repentance.

A midrashic legent indicates that the most precious thing to God is for a person to turn away from wrong and choose the good.

In Christianity. Three uses of this term are common for Christians. First, sin is spiritual or moral failure. It consists of failure to live up to God's requirements, expectations, commandments.

Secondly, sin is active rebellion against God -- intentional, willful revolt.

Thirdly, sin is alienation or estrangement from God. Here sin is a condition, of which specific acts, or "sins," are only manifestations. It is this basic estrangement from God to which Christians refer when they speak of "original sin." Since such a condition cannot be remedied by mankind trapped within it, ultimate deliverance from this condition must be initiated by God.

SUKKOT - The Hebrew name for the Feast of Tabernacles, the word means "booths." In ancient days, it was the custom of the Israelites to live in a sukkah (booth) during the fall harvest. Sukkot is one of the three pilgrimage harvest festivals the Hebrew people are commanded to observe in the Bible. Jews are to celebrate this holiday in remembrance of the time when the Israelites lived in booths as they wandered through the desert. It was a major holiday of the Hebrew people in biblical days and was probably the original Jewish New Year. Sukkot was a harvest festival of thanksgiving, when first-offerings were brought to the Temple in Jerusalem. The American Thanksgiving Day is said to be fashioned after this biblical harvest festival.

Sukkot is celebrated for eight days by traditional Jews in the Diaspora and for seven days, as described in Hebrew Scriptures, by Reform Jews.

SYNAGOGUE - The origins of the synagogue are unknown. During the days of the Second Temple, the synagogue existed in addition to the Temple in Jerusalem.

After the destruction of the Temple, the synagogue became the communal center -- the exclusive place for study, worship and meeting. Eventually the rabbi, as teacher, became the head of the synagogue, performing a role different from that of the Priest in the Temple.

The synagogue is a community of worshipers, who have all learned to read and study Hebrew Scriptures. Since each member is educated, services may be conducted by any member. In the past, membership status was generally reserved for men. Today Reform Judaism recognizes women as full members of the synagogue and lay women as well as rabbis may conduct services.

Traditionally, synagogues are built so that the congregation may face Jerusalem while praying.

TALMUD - The word means "study." Next to Hebrew Scriptures, the Talmud is considered the most authoritative source of Jewish law.

The Talmud consists of several divisions:

  Midrash - which consists of the first interpretations of Mosaic Law after the Torah was canonized (400-200 B.C.E.), consisting of rules, discussions, interpretations and commentaries.

  Mishnah - composed of Halachah, or Law, and Aggadah, which consisted of history, ethics, folklore, etc. (200 B.C.E. to 200 C.E.)

Gemara - Both the Palestinian and the Babylonian Gemara consisted of Halachah, Aggadah and Midrash. The Palestinian Talmud was edited in 425 C.E. and the Babylonian Talmud, which is considered authoritative, received its final editing in 500 C.E.

TEMPLE - The central place of sacrificial worship and the religious center of the Jews in biblical days from the time of King Solomon until 70 C.E.

The Western Wall, previously called the Wailing Wall, is the remaining part of the Temple compound built during the time of Herod the Great. Jews revere the spot and continue to pray there.

TEFILLIN - Two black leather cubes with long leather straps which are worn by traditional male Jews over thirteen years of age during the morning prayer except on the Sabbath and holidays.

"Shel Yad" is placed on the left arm facing the heart and the leather straps are wound seven times around the left arm. "Shel Rosh" is placed on the center of the forehead.

These cases contain passages from the Torah, notably the Sh'ma, written on strips of parchment. They are worn to remind Jews to follow the biblical command to study and obey Torah every day.

TORAH - Means "teaching." The term is most generally used in reference to the first Five Books of Hebrew Scriptures -- Genesis, Exodus, Leviticus, Numbers and Deuteronomy.

A different portion, called a Sidra, is read at each Shabbat service so that the entire Torah is covered in one year.

Torah is also a generic term meaning all teachings of Judaism regarding law, ethics and ritual.

YOM KIPPUR - Hebrew meaning "Day of Atonement." This is a fast day for Jews who, in their synagogues, ask God for forgiveness for the wrongs they committed during the past year. One of the most famous communal prayers, "Al Het," is a long confession of almost every possible sin. Jews fast on Yom Kippur as an act of devotion and purification so that they may concentrate on turning away from any spiritual shortcomings of the past year and determine to live up to the ideals of Judaism in the future. In biblical days, the High Priest confessed the sins for the people and made a special sacrifice -- one goat for God and one goat, called the scapegoat, which was symbolically laden with the sins of the Jewish people, and driven off. Since the destruction of the Second Temple, the Jewish people confess their own sins. Repentance, prayer and tzedakah, an act of righteousness, replaced sacrifices as methods of atonement.

Deicide and the Jews

In the House of Deputies, on the seventh day, the Very Rev. Gray M. Blandy, D.D. of Texas, presented Report No. 6 of the Committee on Ecumenical Relations:

Your Committee on Ecumenical Relations, to whom was referred HD 26, reports as follows:

The Committee has considered the Memorial from the Diocese of Long Island on Christian-Jewish Dialogue and offers the following resolution:

WHEREAS, within the Church, throughout the centuries, loveless attitudes including the charge of deicide, have frequently resulted in persecution of the Jewish people and a concomitant revulsion on the part of the Jewish people towards the un-Christ-like witness thus made; and

WHEREAS, obedience to the Lord of the Church requires an honest and clear expression of love for our neighbor; and

WHEREAS, persecution of the Jews has been recently intensified in certain areas of the world; and

WHEREAS, lack of communication between Christians and Jews, and the resulting ignorance and suspicion of each other, has been a barrier to Christian obedience to the Law of Love; be

RESOLVED, the House of Bishops concurring, that the General Convention of the Protestant Episcopal Church in the United States of America, meeting in St. Louis in October 1964, reject the charge of deicide against the Jews and condemn anti-Semitism; and be it further

RESOLVED, the House of Bishops concurring, that the General Convention condemn unchristian accusations against the Jews; and that this Church seek positive dialogue with appropriate representative bodies of the Jewish faith; and be it further

RESOLVED, the House of Bishops concurring, that the substance of this resolution be referred to the Joint Commission on Ecumenical Relations for continuing study and suggested implementation.

Adopted by the House. Communicated to the House of Bishops by Message No. 55. The House of Bishops received the House of Deputies Message No. 55, condemning unchristian accusations against the Jews.

On motion, the House concurred.

Passed by General Convention of the Episcopal Church, 1964.

Excerpts from Vatican Council Declaration on the Relation
of the Church to Non-Christian Religions

Promulgated by Pope Paul, October 28, 1965

As Holy Scripture testifies, Jerusalem did not recognize the time of her
visitation, nor did the Jews, in large number, accept the Gospel; indeed
not a few opposed its spreading. Nevertheless, God holds the Jews most
dear for the sake of their fathers: He does not repent of the gifts He
makes or of the calls He issuess -- such is the witness of the Apostle.
In company with the prophets and the same Apostle, the Church awaits
that day, known to God alone, on which all peoples will address the
Lord in a single voice and "serve Him shoulder to shoulder" (Soph. 3,9).

Since the spiritual patrimony common to Christians and Jews is thus so
great, this Sacred Synod wants to foster and recommend that mutual
understanding and respect which is the fruit, above all, of biblical and
theological studies as well as of fraternal dialogues.

True, the Jewish authorities and those who followed their lead pressed
for the death of Christ; still, what happened in His passion cannot be
charged against all the Jews, without distinction, then alive nor
against the Jews of today. Although the Church is the new people of
God, the Jews should not be presented as rejected by God or accursed,
as if this followed from the Holy Scriptures. All should see to it,
then, that in catechetical work or in the preaching of the word of God,
they do not teach anything that does not conform to the truth of the
Gospel and the spirit of Christ.

Furthermore, in her rejection of every persecution against any man, the
Church, mindful of the patrimony she shares with the Jews and moved not
by political reasons but by the Gospel's spiritual love, decries hatred,
persecutions, displays of anti-Semitism directed against Jews at any
time and by anyone.

Besides, as the Church has always held and holds now, Christ underwent
His passion and death freely, because of the sins of men and out of
infinite love, in order that all may reach salvation. It is, therefore, the burden of the Church's preaching to proclaim the cross of
Christ as the sign of God's all-embracing love and as the fountain from
which every grace flows.

(New York Times, October 29, 1965)

Taken from the Diocese of Long Island Journal
of the 105th Annual Convention, 1972

Commission on Christian and Jewish Relations

The issue selected for particular attention in 1971 was the place of the land of Palestine in Christian and Jewish thought and the controversial problems centering around the State of Israel. The result of the commission's work on this issue was a lecture and panel-forum on June 1, 1971 on the topic, "A Christian Considers Israel." The principal speaker was the Rev. Karl Baehr, whose topic was, "What foundation can Christians find in their own tradition for their support of the State of Israel?" The responding panel consisted of Mrs. Annette Daum, member of the Executive Board of the New York Federation of Reform Synagogues; the Hon. Eugene Nickerson, formerly County Executive of Nassau County; Dr. Herbert H. Stroup, Professor of Sociology, Brooklyn College; and Rabbi James A. Rudin, Assistant Director of the Interreligious Affairs Department of the American Jewish Committee.

On the basis of this experience, the commission makes the following recommendations to members of the Diocese of Long Island:

1. We should be keenly aware that while Christians are apt to view questions about the State of Israel as primarily political, Jews are more apt to view them as religious ones.

2. We should bear in mind that Christians are likely to underestimate to a very considerable degree the extent of emotional involvement of Jews in all questions regarding the State of Israel.

3. We should hold constantly in mind, in all discussions about the State of Israel, that for the Jew the survival of Israel is equivalent to the survival of Judaism. This is true even for Jews who have no plans ever to move to Israel.

4. In all discussions concerning the State of Israel, Christians must exercise extreme care to ferret out hidden or disguised anti-Semitic implications.

5. Christian (and Jewish) determination to see that Israel survives does not constitute a blanket endorsement of all policies of the Israeli government.

6. Christians should not be misled into making a false analogy between U.S. support of Israel and the situation in Vietnam. The situations are not analogous.

Along the way, the commission has expressed its mind on issues of immediate concern, especially the Soviet oppression of Jews, and has been represented at meetings of other Christian and Jewish organizations concerned with the relations between Christians and Jews.

Respectfully submitted,
The Rev. Robert H. Platman, Chairman

Bibliography

Abraham Our Father in Faith: A Religion Teacher's Curriculum Guide.
Philadelphia: Anti-Defamation League of B'nai B'rith and National
Conference of Catholic Bishops, 1979.

Boadt, Lawrence, Croner, Helga, Klenicki, Leon, ed. Biblical Studies:
Meeting Ground of Jews and Christians. New York: Paulist Press/
Stimulus, 1980.

Croner, Helga, and Leon Klenicki, eds. Issues in the Jewish-Christian
Dialogue: Jewish Perspectives on Covenant, Mission and Witness.
New York: Paulist Press/Stimulus, 1979.

Dahl, Nils Alstrup. The Crucified Messiah and Other Essays. Minneapolis: Augsburg Publishing House, 1974.

Davies, Alan T., ed. Anti-Semitism and the Foundations of Christianity.
New York: Paulist Press, 1979.

Fisher, Eugene T. Faith Without Prejudice. New York: Paulist Press,
1977.

Glock, Charles Y., and Rodney Stark. Christian Beliefs and Anti-Semitism. New York: Harper Torchbooks, 1966.

Isaac, Jules. The Teaching of Contempt: Christian Roots of Anti-Semitism. New York: Holt, Rinehart and Winston, 1964.

Kaufman, Harriet L. Jews and Judaism Since Jesus: An Introduction.
Cincinnati: Kaufman House Publishers, 1978.

McCoombe, Lawrence, ed. Ecumenical Bulletin #44, a Special Jewish-
Christian Edition. Ecumenical Office of the Episcopal Church, New
York, 1980.

Pawlikowski, John T. Sinai and Calvary: A Meeting of Two Peoples.
Beverly Hills, California: Benziger, 1976.

_____. What Are They Saying About Christian-Jewish Rela-
tions? New York: Paulist Press, 1980.

Ruether, Rosemary Radford. Faith and Fratricide: The Theological Roots
of Anti-Semitism. New York: Seabury Press, 1974.

Sandmel, Samuel. Anti-Semitism in the New Testament? Philadelphia:
Fortress Press, 1978.

_____. We Jews and Jesus. New York: Oxford University
Press, 1973.

Schauss, Hayyim. Guide to Jewish Holy Days. New York: Schocken Books,
1962.

Sloyan, Gerard S. <u>Jesus on Trial</u>. Philadelphia: Fortress Press, 1973.

Spong, John Shelby and Jack Daniel Spiro. <u>Dialogue: In Search of Jewish-Christian Understanding</u>. New York: Seabury/Crossroads, 1975.

Strober, Gerald S. <u>Portrait of the Elder Brother: Jews and Judaism in Protestant Teaching Materials</u>. New York: American Jewish Committee and National Conference of Christians and Jews, 1972.

Talmage, F.E., ed. <u>Disputation and Dialogue: Readings in the Jewish-Christian Encounter</u>. New York: Ktav and Anti-Defamation League of B'nai B'rith, 1975.

Thoma, Clemens. <u>A Christian Theology of Judaism</u>. New York: Paulist Press, Stimulus, 1980.

Townsend, John T. <u>A Liturgical Interpretation of Our Lord's Passion in Narrative Form</u>. New York: National Conference of Christians and Jews, 1977.

Wilson, William R. <u>The Execution of Jesus</u>. New York: Scribner's, 1970.

Texts for Children

<u>Jesus Goes to School</u> by Carrie Lou Goddard
<u>Jesus Goes to the Synagogue</u> by Helen Brown
<u>Jesus Lights the Sabbath Lamp</u> by James S. Tippett
The above are published by Abingdon Press, New York.

For High School and Youth

<u>Our Religion and our Neighbors</u> by Milton G. Miller and Sylvan D. Schwartzman, UAHC, revised edition.
This is a text for young Jewish people on comparative religion, prepared with the help of authorities of the major faiths in this country. The book discusses Roman Catholicism, Protestantism, Judaism, Eastern Orthodoxy, Islam, Hinduism, Buddhism and Confucianism.

Magazines for Upper Grades

<u>Keeping Posted</u> (available from the Union of American Hebrew Congregations)
    "Judaism and Christianity: Parting of the Ways" #840260
    "Righteous Gentiles" #840640
    "Aspects of the Holocaust" #840440
    "Zionism" #840450
    "The Hebrew Bible" #840200

SOME THOUGHTS ON OFFICIATION

1. "We believe that intermarriage is neither good nor bad, just as we believe that the marriage between two Jews, in itself, is neither good nor bad. The moral worth of a marriage always depends on the quality of the human relationship ... We believe that rabbis who officiate at intermarriage ceremonies demonstate their commitment to human freedom, dignity and love. We hope that more rabbis will choose to affirm these values." (Society for Humanistic Judaism).

2. "The C.C.A.R., recalling its stand adopted in 1909 "that mixed marriage is contrary to the Jewish tradition and should be discouraged," now declares its opposition to participation by its members in any ceremony which solemnizes a mixed marriage... The C.C.A.R. recognizes that historically its members have held and continue to hold divergent interpretations of Jewish history. (CCAR 1973).

3. "(Intermarriage) represents a potential drain on the numeric strength of the Jewish people and on its inner commitment. Whether I like it or not, my officiation would be seen as a seal of approval and would, therefore, become encouraging of intermarriage." (R. Alexander Schindler).

4. "Obviously there is a great satisfaction in meeting the needs of the couples, but when at least two-thirds of my marriages are mixed marriages, I've got to wonder what it says to the Confirmation child or Bar Mitzvah about carrying on Judaism? I can't forget David Einhorn's classic line that mixed marriage is the nail in the coffin of Judaism. It haunts me." (R. Ken Segal).

5. "It finally dawned on me that sometimes a given mixed marriage may actually serve the interests of the Jewish community... There are clearly situations in which mixed marriages will result in Jewish continuity and will strengthen the fabric of Jewish life. In such situations, I would argue that rabbis should be present for these couples, playing the role of mekarev, drawing them near to Judaism and the Jewish people, not estranging or rejecting them. The unfortunate aspect of this posture is it means that we need to assess each relationship on its Jewish merits. The role of assessor is downright uncomfortable. For the sake of Judaism and the Jewish people, however, it surpasses the more categorical position." (Meditiations of a Maverick Rabbi, by R. Al Axelrad).

6.   "... as long as the Jewish partner had a firm commitment
     to Judaism, the couple intended to have a Jewish home
     and the non-Jewish partner has no conflicting faith
     commitment." (R. Edgar Magnin).

7.   "When officiating at a marriage ceremony, the rabbi acts as
     representative of the Jewish people and the Jewish heritage.
     What the rabbi does or does not do has an effect on the
     totality of Jewry and on our people's potential for sur-
     vival in the midst of an over-whelmingly non-Jewish society."
     (Committee of 100).

8.   "Certainly we as Reform Jews must state boldly and clearly,
     as we have numerous times declared, that in all cases in-
     volving the relationship of Jew and non-Jew, interfaith
     marriage, or the status of the children of such unions, the
     talmudic halakha is not operative. It is null and void. It
     is not dat Moshe weYisrael. Its principles cannot, must not,
     be used. It is contrary to the higher impulses of traditional
     Judaism itself, contrary to the demands of God as Judaism per-
     ceives them. The literal halakha in this total area must be
     categorically rejected." (Responsa on Jewish Marriage, by
     R. Eugene Mihaly).

OFFICIATION

Some Questions and Answers

Any discussion on the issue of the rabbinic offficiation of intermarriages must be preceded by a reminder that the ultimate policy guidelines are generated by the Central Conference of American Rabbis and individual rabbis then decide what their particular policy will be. The following is an attempt to respond to some questions which are frequently raised concerning this complex issue. The issue of rabbinic officiation is outside the purview of the Commission on Reform Jewish Outreach.

1. What was the Central Conference of American Rabbis' 1973 resolution of the Committee on Mixed Marriage?

The C.C.A.R., recalling its stand adopted in 1909 "that mixed marriage is contrary to the Jewish tradition and should be discouraged," now declares its opposition to participation by its members in any ceremony which solemnizes a mixed marriage.

The C.C.A.R. recognizes that historically its members have held and continue to hold divergent interpretations of Jewish tradition.

In order to keep open every channel to Judaism and K'lal Yisrael for those who have already entered into mixed marriage, the C.C.A.R. calls upon its members:

- to assist fully in educating children of such mixed marriages as Jews;

- to provide the opportunity for conversion of the non-Jewish spouse; and

- to encourage a creative and consistent cultivation of involvement in the Jewish community and the synagogue.

2. What are some of the arguments advanced by the Subcommittee on Mixed Marriage to the Task Force on Reform Jewish Outreach in favor of Rabbinic Officiation?

a) Rabbinic officiation at intermarriages enhances the possibility that children will be raised as Jews and the non-Jewish spouse will be more likely to consider the possibility of conversion at some later date.

b) When a rabbi refuses to officiate at an intermarriage, the couple may be alientated from the synagogue. The person of another faith, or of no professed faith, who requests that a rabbi officiate at his/her marriage has already made a first, positive decision toward Judaism.

c) A refusal to officiate cannot be reconciled with Reform

Judaism's emphasis upon interfaith dialogue and the prophetic message of universal brotherhood.

d) Rabbis can create wedding ceremonies appropriate to the occasion rather than utilizing the traditional Jewish ritual.

e) It is time to stop being concerned at the reactions of Orthodox and Conservative Judaism to the practices of Reform. Over the years, Reform Judaism has made numerous decisions which contravene Jewish law. In our pluralistic society, a significant percentage of Jews now marry persons born outside our faith. These marriages are increasing regardless of the rabbinic stance. We cannot afford to reject such a large proportion of our young people and their parents.

f) Both the 1973 C.C.A.R. resolution and the statements found in the Rabbis Manual have exerted powerful pressures upon rabbis to refrain from officiating at intermarriages lest in doing so they jeopardize their futures as members of that body.

g) Outreach begins before a marriage takes place. An outreach program which is intent upon reaching out to couples in an intermarriage but which disapproves of rabbinic officiation at intermarriages is a contradiction in terms.

h) Rabbis should be permitted to officiate at intermarriages in the sanctuary of the congregation. Such an act would increase the chances of the non-Jewish partner's conversion to Judaism.

3. What are some of the arguments advanced by the Subcommittee on Mixed Marriage to the Task Force on Reform Jewish Outreach in opposition to Rabbinic Officiation?

a) Premarital promises regarding the religious upbringing of children are prone to change subsequent to the birth of a child. Often commitments to educate children as Jews or to convert oneself are not voluntary but concessions to pressure brought to bear by the Jewish partner and the Jewish partner's family.

b) A growing number of intermarried couples have affiliated with synagogues and are raising their children as Jews despite the fact they were not married by a rabbi.

c) The preservation of one's particular Jewish identity is both consistent and necessary if the integrity of other cultures, ethnic groups and faith communities is to be defended.

d) The rabbi is the symbolic representative of Judaism and of the continuity of the Jewish tradition. To tailor ritual to fit the religious needs of the couple is to subvert the basic assumptions under which both Judaism and the State have granted the rabbi the perogative to serve as an officiant in the first place. The rabbi's participation in the ceremony is construed by the Jewish partner and the Jewish family as a sign that the wedding is a

Jewish wedding thereby assuaging the family's discomfiture at the reality of an intermarriage.

e) It is not a question of Reform versus Orthodox interpretations of Judaism. It is a question of Jewish survival and the sanction of behavior which violates the purpose and meaning of Jewish marriage and rabbinic responsibility.

f) The C.C.A.R. has always permitted the free exchange of positions and points of view. The 1973 resolution clearly recognizes that members may hold divergent views regarding officiating at intermarriages.

g) The Outreach program stands on its own merits. There is no inconsistency whatsoever in a program designed to deal with the religious needs of couples after their marriage and the affirmation that a Jewish marriage is involving men and women who are committed to Judaism as a personal way of life.

h) To solemnize a wedding between a Jew and a non-Jew in a synagogue sanctuary is to transform a sacred moment in the life cycle of the Jewish people into an act of hypocricy.

4) Where can further information be obtained regarding the on-going rabbinic debate on officiation?

a) The "Committee of 100" published a booklet entitled "Reform Rabbis and Mixed Marriage," on why rabbis should not officiate at intermarriages. A copy of this booklet can be obtained by writing to: "Committee of 100," Congregation Keneseth Israel, Old York Road at Township Line, Elkins Park, PA 19117

b) Rabbi Eugene Mihaly's <u>Teshuvot(Responsa) on Jewish Marriage</u> (Cincinnati, Ohio 1985), which suggests that support for rabbinic officiation can be found within the rabbinic tradition, is a response to the statement of the "Committee of 100."

5) What about synagogue policies regarding the participation of non-Jewish members in various rituals, on committees, the Board of Trustees, etc.?

A suggested constitution and by-laws for congregations affiliated with the Union of American Hebrew Congregations was adopted by the Joint Commission on Synagogue Administration of the U.A.H.C. and the C.C.A.R. in 1968, and amended in 1970 and 1984. A copy of these guidelines can be obtained through the U.A.H.C.

6) Some questions for consideration:

* What factors lead to intermarriage?

* Do you feel a non-Jewish spouse is capable of creating a Jewish home and nurturing Jewish children?

* How does intermarriage affect Jewish solidarity and continuity?

* How does intermarriage affect the quality of one's Jewishness?

A Summary of the Report of the Joint UAHC/CCAR Task Force on Reform Jewish Outreach

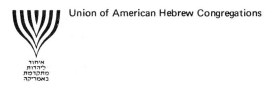

Union of American Hebrew Congregations

איחוד
ליהדות
מתקדמת
באמריקה

August 31, 1981

Dear Rabbis and Members of UAHC Congregations:

Approximately two and one-half years ago, I was asked to serve as Chairman of the Joint UAHC/CCAR Task Force on Reform Jewish Outreach. I accepted this responsibility because I am an American Jew and believe that it is vitally important for the future of my country and for the future of Judaism that there continue to be a strong, vibrant Jewish community in the United States in the centuries ahead. I also believe that a program of Reform Jewish Outreach can be a major factor in helping attain this goal.

We American Jews have received so much from this wonderful land of freedom and opportunity, and we have given so much in return. One shudders to think what the United States would be like today if it had not opened its borders for the immigration of oppressed Jews.

But great as our contributions have been in the past, they can be even greater in the future. In large part, this will depend upon whether we Jews will be able to adapt to our continually changing environment as we have done in the past. Our very survival over thousands of years - one of the most unique chapters in the history of mankind - is vivid testimony to the strength of our religious roots and our heritage. Yet, we are now faced with a new challenge brought about by a combination of circumstances, including accelerating change in our society, ever-diminishing barriers of discrimination accompanied by increased assimilation, diminishing birth rates, and a tremendous increase in the number of marriages between people who are Jewish by birth and those who are not. Many of the partners in those marriages choose to become Jews. However, others have not chosen Judaism - often because they were never asked.

At the same time that we Jews are seeking answers to the questions
raised by these new conditions, non-Jewish Americans who have no
religious preference are also seeking to meet their own personal
religious needs and goals. Might Judaism be one of the alternatives
these religiously non-preferenced Americans consider in their quest
for peace of mind and soul? An increasing number of Jews believe
that we should - at the very least - enable these people to learn
more about Judaism, including the fact that Reform Judaism does welcome
men and women who might want to become Jews.

There is also increased concern about four other major areas of
Outreach: The needs of, and programs for -- the non-Jewish partner
in a mixed marriage; children of mixed marriages; people who have
already decided to seek conversion to Judaism; and persons who have
recently converted to Judaism.

It is within this frame of reference that the Task Force on Reform
Jewish Outreach embarked upon its study. Our group of 26 rabbis,
UAHC Trustees, and other lay leaders have worked very hard with great
dedication to try and find answers to the many questions that have
been raised. Although we came from a wide variety of backgrounds and
experiences and have had many differing points of view, we ultimately
were able to arrive at a unanimous agreement.

Our conclusions and the resolutions that we propose to offer at the
1981 UAHC Biennial Convention in Boston in December are included in
the Summary of our Report, a copy of which is enclosed. (If you would
care to have a copy of the entire Report, it can be purchased for $10
from the UAHC.)

We hope you will give much thought and study to the enclosed Summary
of our Report and that your delegates to the 1981 Biennial will be
prepared to vote on the formal resolutions that we propose. We do
not expect that every person will agree with all of our findings and
recommendations. But we hope everyone will recognize that we undertook our work in an atmosphere of full and frank discussion in the
greatest tradition of our faith.

Truly, we are at one of the major crossroads in the history of the
Jews. The direction that we take will have a tremendous impact on
our future and on the future of our country. It will be up to each
of us to help lead the way.

Sincerely,

David W. Belin, Chairman
Task Force on Reform Jewish Outreach

August 31, 1981

Mr. Donald S. Day, Chairman
UAHC Board of Trustees
Union of American Hebrew Congregations
838 Fifth Avenue
New York NY 10021

Dear Donald:

On behalf of the Joint Union of American Hebrew
Congregations/Central Conference of American Rabbis
Task Force on Reform Jewish Outreach, I am pleased
to submit our final Report.

Sincerely,

David W. Belin, Chairman
Task Force on Reform Jewish Outreach

A SUMMARY OF THE REPORT OF THE JOINT

UAHC/CCAR TASK FORCE ON REFORM JEWISH OUTREACH

David W. Belin, Chairman
Rabbi Max Shapiro, Co-Chairman
Rabbi Sanford Seltzer, Director of
    Special Projects and UAHC Coordinator

Stanley J. Beskind
Carl Feldman
Robert Hess
Mary Lynn Kotz
Constance Kreshtool
Lydia Kukoff
Seymour M. Liebowitz
Ira Lipman
Lillian Maltzer
Rabbi Bernard Mehlman
Melvin Merians
Rabbi Eugene Mihaly

Lucille Miller
Rabbi Burton Padoll
Josephine Narva
Jocelyn Rudner
Lawrence Sachnowitz
Rabbi Robert J. Schur
Elizabeth V. L. Stern
Paul Uhlmann, Jr.
Rabbi Sheldon Zimmerman
EX OFFICIO
Rabbi Joseph Glaser
Rabbi Daniel B. Syme

August, 1981

PREFACE

The organization of the Joint Union of American Hebrew Congregations-Central Conference of American Rabbis Task Force on Reform Jewish Outreach grew out of a remarkable address by Rabbi Alexander Schindler, President of the Union of American Hebrew Congregations. On December 2, 1978, shortly after our country was horrified by the Jonestown massacre, Rabbi Schindler spoke before a meeting of the UAHC Board of Trustees. He called for consideration of an Outreach Program so that Judaism could "respond openly and positively to those God-seekers who voluntarily ask for our knowledge . . .

> "Millions of Americans are searching for something. Tragically -- as the grisly events of the past week have established -- many of these seekers have fallen prey to mystical cults which literally enslave them.
>
> "Well, Judaism offers life, not death. It teaches free will, not surrender of body and soul to another human being. The Jew prays directly to God, not through an intermediary who stands between him and his God. Judaism is a religion of hope and not despair, it insists that man and society are perfectible. Judaism has an enormous amount of wisdom and experience to offer this troubled world, and we Jews ought to be proud to speak about it, frankly, freely, and with dignity."

The UAHC Board of Trustees adopted a resolution at that December 2, 1978, meeting calling for the appointment of a Task Force to study the entire area of Outreach. David W. Belin, a member of the UAHC Board of Trustees and an attorney from Des Moines, Iowa, was appointed as Chairman of the Task Force. His background included leadership in the Jewish community as well as national public service. In 1964, he served as counsel to the Warren Commission, which investigated the assassination of President Kennedy. In 1975, President Ford appointed him Executive Director of the Rockefeller Commission, which investigated the CIA.

In agreeing to accept the appointment as Task Force Chairman, David Belin said: "We American Jews are concerned about the need for a healthy, vital American Jewish community because we are Americans and because we are Jews. It would be a tragedy for the Jewish people if there were not a vibrant Jewish community in America. It would also be a tragedy for America, and indeed for the world, if there were not a strong, vibrant Jewish community in the United States. I believe that a program of Reform Jewish Outreach can be a major factor in helping attain this goal. This is the primary reason that I have agreed to accept this reponsibility."

The CCAR asked to join in the overall effort, and Rabbi Max Shapiro of Minneapolis, Chairman of the CCAR Conversion Committee, was appointed as Task Force Co-Chairman. Twenty-four other Reform Jews, including rabbis, UAHC Trustees, and other Reform lay leaders were appointed to the Task Force. The group included men and women who were themselves Jews by choice; many others had personal experiences within their families or among close friends which gave them added insight. Rabbi Sanford Seltzer of the UAHC staff served as the Director of Special Projects for the Task Force and worked closely with Chairman David Belin in the coordination of the overall study. Rabbi Seltzer also wrote the preliminary draft of the final Report. The Summary of the Report was prepared by Chairman David Belin and Rabbi Seltzer.

There were five major areas of inquiry, each of which was assigned to a Task Force subcommittee. Four of these areas involved a study of the needs of and programs for -- the non-Jewish partner in a mixed marriage; the children of mixed marriages; people who have already decided to seek conversion to Judaism; and people who have been recently converted to Judaism. The fifth area of inquiry concentrated on whether or not there should be a Reform Jewish Outreach program to the millions of Americans of no religious preference. Several of these areas had been included in a 1973 CCAR Resolution which called upon its members to assist in the education of children of mixed marriages as Jews, to provide the opportunity for conversion of the non-Jewish spouse, and to encourage the involvement of the mixed-married family in the Jewish community and the synagogue.

We began with a study of the history of Jewish conversion efforts, going back to Biblical traditions and continuing into the post-Biblical period up to the present day. The Task Force assembled and analyzed background materials including the philosophical, cultural and sociological aspects of the ethical teachings and message of Judaism; the uniqueness of Jewish survival in world history, including an examination of some of the reasons for this historical phenomenon; and the Jewish contribution to the development of the United States, ranging from the influence of Jewish ethical values to the contributions of Jews to society as a whole in the areas of the arts, education, philanthropy, government and law, human rights, medicine, science, social justice and others.

We also examined the impact that an Outreach program might have on the American Jewish community, including marriages where one partner is a Jew by choice, mixed marriages, the collateral benefits to Jews in teaching non-Jews about Judaism, and the social and political consequences for Jews and non-Jews of the continuing diminution of the percentage of Americans who are Jews. In addition, we analyzed the importance of a Reform Jewish Outreach program to the entire world Jewish community, including in particular the importance of such a program to the State of Israel.

Our study also included an examination of existing Jewish programs which were relevant to the work of the Task Force. These included programs of primary and secondary school education, camping programs, adult and family education programs, and programs of other Jewish groups which might have an impact in the area. We then undertook a specific study of the various aspects of programs of Reform Jewish Outreach.

Although initially there was wide divergence of opinion among the members of the Task Force, we ultimately came to consensus in our overall conclusions, and we unanimously adopted five formal resolutions which we are recommending for adoption by the Union of American Hebrew Congregations at its 1981 Biennial Convention in Boston commencing on December 3.

Before turning to these formal conclusions and the resolutions adopted by the Task Force, it is important to examine some of the highlights of the historical perspective which formed a part of the foundation of our study.

JEWS AND CONVERSION: A HISTORIC PERSPECTIVE

The people of Israel were bound to God by a unique, immutable covenant, a "brit olam." Under the terms of this covenant, it became our destiny to bring the ethical imperatives of the Jewish faith to the four corners of the earth. Judaism's message of love, truth and justice was intended to encompass all of humankind. Indeed, the system of morals and ethics born of Judaism is the cornerstone of western civilization.

The triumph of Judaism is the survival of the Jewish people and the Jewish faith for nearly four thousand years - perhaps the most miraculous survival in the history of humankind. The reasons for our survival are inherent in the strengths of the faith. Judaism is life-enhancing, rather than life-denying. It has a rich, joyful and beautiful tradition. It is humanistic and compassionate, with a commitment to care for the poor and the oppressed. Judaism reveres education, it encourages questioning. It offers spiritual nourishment for humankind, in worship of the living God.

Judaism has survived not only because its people have kept the covenant with God but also because it has ever enriched its ancient strengths with new thought, and because it has followed its ancient imperative to bring people in.

The Biblical Period

Throughout Biblical times, seeking out the new believer was a tenet of our faith. As God explained to Moses, "I am the God who brings near, and does not push away." Ancient Judaism taught: "So you, when someone comes to you, draw him nigh. Do not push him away." In Leviticus, it is written, "Love the stranger, because you were strangers in Egypt."

Those who came to Judaism were honored. Two of the tribes of Israel are descended from the wife of Joseph, a daughter of Egypt's high priest. Moses, the great law-giver himself, chose a non-Israelite as his wife. Ruth, the Moabite, chose Judaism with the words repeated by converts today: "Thy people shall be my people, thy God, my God." Her legacy was the dynasty of King David of whom the messiah was promised.

The mission of Judaism, under the terms of the covenant, was to be accomplished by both personal and collective example. Jews were to inspire others to link their destiny with the Jewish people, or to live in accordance with Judaism's message of love, truth and justice.

"Behold my covenant is with you and you shall be the father of a multitude of nations," God instructs Abraham in Genesis 17, "and I will establish my covenant between me and you and your descendants after you throughout their generations for an everlasting covenant."

To the prophets, particularly Isaiah, Israel was the divine instrument for perfecting the world under the kingdom of the Almighty:

"I the Lord have called thee for a covenant of the people for a light unto the nations." "It is too light a thing that you should be my servant to raise up the tribes of Jacob and to restore the preserved of Israel. I will give you as a light to the nations that my salvation may reach to the end of the earth." (Isaiah 42 and 49.)

Isaiah fervently believed in Israel's mission as a universal faith and looked to the day when all would assemble at God's holy mountain and when God's house would be called "a house of prayer for all peoples." Zechariah also echoed this message.

The mission of Judaism as a comprehensive, universal faith is further stated in the Book of Jonah. On Yom Kippur, the holiest day of the Jewish year, Jews read of God punishing Jonah for refusing to preach to the people of Nineveh. This part of the liturgy is to remind us of our mission as Jews.

The prophetic tradition championed the ideal of ethical monotheism and spoke of a God whose dominion transcended national boundaries, whose moral imperatives were incumbent upon all peoples. This led to the emergence of Judaism as a universal faith, whose God was the God of all nations and to whom the people of Israel were bound by an immutable convenant.

Israel's mission as a covenant people was realized not only when non-Jews embraced Judaism but also by the code of ethics affirmed by other world religions founded upon Judaism's concept of ethical monotheism.

The Post-Biblical Period

During the Talmudic period, the dominant attitude of Judaism was overwhelmingly positive toward reaching out and welcoming converts. This attitude is reported in Rabbinic literature, Greek and Roman and early Christian sources. Many Talmudic stories speak of the reverence with which the task of converting the stranger was to be conducted. Men and women who chose to become Jews were called "those who seek shelter under

-122-

the shade of God." The rabbis wrote: "They shall flourish like corn; they shall blossom like the vine." And" "Proselytes are as dear to me as the wine which is poured out upon the altar" (of the Temple).

Serious efforts at missionizing fostered the spread of Judaism during Greco-Roman times. The world Jewish population increased from between one-half to one million in the year 440 B.C.E. to between two and five million in the first century, C.E. However, these proselytizing efforts were halted by the edict of Constantine in the fourth century, establishing Christianity as the official state religion of the Empire. To convert to Judaism became a capital offense. Yet, the Roman Empire collapsed, and Judaism survived.

During medieval times, rabbis were favorable both to conversion and to converts. There were many episodes of mass conversions despite the Crusades, despite intermittent repression. In the fourteenth century, Rabbi Simeon Duran in Spain enumerated all 613 Commandments. This time, "To seek out the convert," was listed, not as a subsection of "Thou Shalt Love the Lord," but as a separate Commandment in its own right.

The Spanish Inquisition, however, reinstituted capital punishment for the "crime" of conversion to Judaism. That action, along with the Inquisition's aggressive pursuit of heresy and a general anti-Semitic atmosphere in Europe, served as powerful deterrents to Jewish efforts at seeking converts during the centuries that followed. A tradition of not seeking converts was developed and, instead, emphasis was placed upon the Talmudic principle that all persons who adhered to the laws of Noah had a place in the world to come. In stark contrast to the way many Muslims and Christians looked upon Judaism, Jews accepted Islam and Christianity as valid religions.

The divine vocation of the Jewish people has been a conspicuous theme in American Reform Judaism from its beginnings. Reform scholars and leaders - Rabbis Samuel Holdheim, Isaac Mayer Wise, Kaufman Kohler and David Einhorn, as well as Stephen Wise and Maurice Eisendrath - shared that ideal, and beginning with Isaac Mayer Wise in 1849, Reform leaders made numerous proposals to return to our ancient tradition and to initiate Outreach to Americans who professed no religion.

In that spirit, the editors of the Union Prayer Book included references to the mission of Israel as part of the worship service on the Sabbath and the Day of Atonement, two of the most universal occasions in the festival cycle of the Jewish year. In the waning hours of Yom Kippur the congregation reads: "Grant that the children of Israel may recognize the goal of their changeful career so that

they may exemplify by their zeal and love for humankind the truth
of Israel's message, one humanity on earth even as there is but one
God in heaven."

A similar sentiment inspires the ritual for Sabbath eve:
"Almighty and merciful God, thou hast called Israel to thy service
and found him worthy to bear witness unto thy truth unto the peoples
of the earth. Give us grace to fulfill this mission with zeal
tempered by wisdom and guided by regard for other men's faith."

However, for many reasons, ranging from a misunderstanding
of Jewish historical experience to fears of inciting anti-Semitism
in a world where prejudice and discrimination against Jews was the
rule, the question of Outreach was not extensively debated until
the past few years. The capacity and willingness of Jews to speak
once again of mission and to phrase our destiny in religious terms
in and of itself is of profound significance.

The Torah defines Jews as a "holy people." The miracle of
Jewish survival defies logic and confounds reasoned explanations.
Many rabbis have suggested that the survival of Judaism stands as
unequivocal testimony to the Divine Presence in the process of
history and reaffirms the possibility of a tomorrow in the face of
today's despair. Judaism lives today, as in Biblical times, because
it was founded upon the word of God and because it continues as the
word of God.

Jews As A Barometer of Social Progress and Freedom

History has shown that Jews, perhaps more than any other people
or ethnic community, represent a barometer of the intellectual health
of a nation, of its political viability and its socio-economic
potential.

Wherever Jews were oppressed, persecuted, expelled or destroyed,
whether in medieval Spain under the power of the Inquisition, or
Nazi Germany through Hitler's "final solution," those governments
ultimately led their countries into decline. Wherever Jews lived
peacefully, the citizens of those countries generally enjoyed a
fuller measure of freedom and opportunity. Jews have served as the
conscience of every society of which they have been a part.

The influence of Jewish ethical values and the Judeo-Christian heritage has contributed far more to the development of the United States than is generally recognized. For instance, at the base of our governmental and societal structure are the Ten Commandments and the Jewish covenant with God to keep those Commandments. The elements of justice, love and mercy are inherent in the practice of Judaism. The Jewish concept of charity, our concept of the strength of family and home, and the devotion to learning have been important from the beginning in building America.

Jewish ethical and moral values are inextricably woven into the foundations of America. The right to speak, the right to religious freedom, the right to honest transaction, the right to dissent, the right to be judged by one's peers, and the principles of fairness and concern for the downtrodden - all these and more are basic tenets of Jewish belief that stem from the Bible and are part of the American fabric.

The concerns of the founding fathers for the rights of due process and equal protection under the law, for freedom of speech and religion, and for all of the other fundamental principles set forth in the Constitution and in the Bill of Rights have been of great meaning to Jews. Most Jewish immigrants had known repression and government authoritarianism in the lands from which they came.

No other country in history has afforded the Jews a greater opportunity to realize their full potential than has the United States. The rewards to our country for having opened its doors to Jewish immigrants have been great. No single group has played a more conspicuous role in safeguarding democratic institutions and preserving regard for the inalienable rights of all of its citizens.

Moreover, the contributions to our society by American Jews have been disproportionately far greater than our numbers in the total population would ordinarily indicate. In the arts, in education, in the natural sciences, in the social sciences, in medicine, in law, and public service, Jews have made outstanding achievements which in turn have benefited the entire country. Jewish men and women have also generously supported philanthropic activities throughout our nation. In almost every city in the United States where a significant number of Jews live, they are in the forefront of participation and leadership in civic affairs and charitable endeavors.

Non-Jewish leaders repeatedly comment on how much our American society has benefited because of the extraordinary contributions of Jews in these civic activities. (Although the Task Force concentrated its study on the United States, similar experiences have also occurred in Canada.)

Jews have been called "America's conscience." In the fields of human rights and social justice, Jews have served active leadership roles, organizing social movements that have culminated in major progressive changes in American society.

The presence of Jews and Judaism as vital forces on the American scene cannot be overemphasized. The influence of Jewish Chatauqua lectureships on college campuses in teaching non-Jews about Judaism has built bridges of understanding and cooperation between Jews and non-Jews and has broken down prejudices and stereotypes.

Chairs in Judaism, doctoral programs in Jewish studies, exchange opportunities between American campuses and institutions of higher learning in Israel, and fellowships for Christian seminarians at the Hebrew Union College have been major forces in improving Christian-Jewish relationships here and abroad.

At the same time that the American experience offered an unparalleled opportunity for advancement, America's welcome tended also to secularize the American Jew to a degree unparalleled in Jewish history. The religious aspect of Jewish life was played down - as was that of the Christian community. The breakdown of religious barriers was accompanied by an increasing acceptance of Jews by non-Jews.

The openness of American society is vividly illustrated by the fact that marriages involving Jews and non-Jews are now estimated to be more than one-third of all marriages where there is a Jewish partner. This has been a source of grave concern to the organized American Jewish community.

On the other hand, the choice of Jewish mates by non-Jews is evidence of increasingly open attitudes towards Jews and Judaism. Moreover, the tendency of converts to embrace synagogue life and become practicing, observant Jews, and the infusion of new people into a community experiencing a decreasing birth rate are all healthy signs which should no longer be overlooked or devalued.

The vitality, commitment and inspiration brought to Judaism
by Jews-by-choice have been dramatically demonstrated in the
Conferences (Outreach weekends) on the Needs and Problems of Jews
by Choice sponsored by the Task Force during 1980 and 1981. The
depth of religious commitment by persons who have converted to Judaism
is documented on videotapes made available by the UAHC. When these
Jews by choice have returned to their communities to speak of their
Jewish experience, the response of individual congregations has been
overwhelming. For many congregations, it is the first time that
Jews by birth have heard someone of "outside" origins say that it
is "wonderful" and "all right" to be Jewish. Many born Jews are
thirsty for such statements, and they respond with a reaffirmation
of their own faith.

A recent study by Dr. Steven Huberman entitled "New Jews, the
Dynamics of Religious Conversion", concluded that converts to Judaism
tend to make stronger commitments to Judaism (attendance at religious
services, observance of home rituals, holiday observances) than the
population of born Jews as a whole. These converts have indicated
that their reason for conversion was one of serious, intrinsic
intent. They felt Judaism to be a strong, meaningful faith. Eighty-
six percent of those Jews by choice queried believe it is important
for every Jewish child to be given a continuing Jewish education
so that the "chain of tradition" may continue.

Even in the case of mixed marriages, many non-Jewish spouses
are open to the possibility of a Jewish education for their
children. This is particularly true where the non-Jewish spouse
forges social and cultural ties with the Jewish community. It
is therefore very important to recognize both the reality that
mixed marriages will take place and the opportunity for Jewish
identity of the children of such marriages. This will result in
a realistic appraisal of the situation and will enhance the development of new and constructive programs to meet the needs of the
Jewish community.

Over the years, the Reform movement - through the efforts of
the Union of American Hebrew Congregations and the Central Conference
of American Rabbis - more than any other Jewish religious body, has
addressed the needs and concerns of persons considering conversion
to Judaism and their Jewish partners, as well as the needs of persons
in a mixed-marriage. It was therefore a most logical step for the
Reform Movement to have this Task Force appointed to undertake a
study of an overall program of Reform Jewish Outreach.

TASK FORCE CONCLUSIONS AND PROPOSED RESOLUTIONS

The Task Force adopted the following conclusions and proposes the following formal resolutions for adoption by the 1981 UAHC Biennial:

The Non-Jewish Partner In A Mixed Marriage

The non-Jewish partner in a mixed marriage has special needs. We believe there should be a Reform Jewish Outreach program to help meet these needs. Such programs should take into consideration the situation where the non-Jewish partner has no other religious preference and should also take into consideration those situations where the non-Jewish partner is committed to another religion. In the latter case, where there is commitment to another religion, there should be no attempt to convert that person to Judaism. An Outreach program should bring information about Judaism and the Jewish people to the family and also should be directed toward making that non-Jewish partner feel comfortable in the synagogue and in the entire Jewish community. Within this frame of reference, the Task Force recommends the adoption of the following Resolution:

1. The Task Force On Reform Jewish Outreach believes that the Jewish community should give increased attention to the special needs of the non-Jewish partner in a mixed marriage. The Task Force urges that the Union of American Hebrew Congregations and its member congregations develop programs and educational materials that will welcome these individuals into the community, provide for their special Jewish educational and experiential needs and help them enhance the Jewish content of their family life and create a warm and supportive climate that will encourage them to raise their children as Jews and to choose Judaism as their own personal faith.

The Children of Mixed Marriages

The Task Force believes that there is a great need for a Reform Jewish Outreach program for children of mixed marriages. Judaism has much to offer these children, and through Reform Jewish Outreach programs we would hope to encourage these children to seek a Jewish education and, in any event, to identify themselves as Jews when they reach adulthood. Within this frame of reference, the Task Force urges the adoption of the following Resolution:

2. The Task Force On Reform Jewish Outreach urges the Union of American Hebrew Congregations and its member congregations develop programs and educational materials:

1) <u>To encourage parents in a mixed marriage to enroll their</u> <u>children in a program of Jewish education</u>.

2) <u>To encourage college students and young adults of a</u> <u>mixed-marriage background to freely choose Judaism as</u> <u>their personal faith</u>.

<u>These programs and materials should be so designed to aid</u> <u>in the positive integration of children of mixed marriages</u> <u>into the religious school. They should also be so designed</u> <u>to provide college students and young adults with information</u> <u>and with experiential opportunities enabling them to more</u> <u>fully understand and appreciate the quality of Jewish life</u> <u>and the heritage of the Jewish people</u>.

No discussion of effective programs of Outreach for children of mixed marriages is complete without reference to the issue of matrilineal and patrilineal determinations of Jewish status. Although Orthodox Judaism states that whoever is born of a Jewish mother is Jewish, and denies the Jewishness of a child whose father is Jewish and whose mother is not, Reform Judaism, as a result of the farsighted decision of the Central Conference of American Rabbis, is on record as asserting that it "accepts such a child as Jewish without a formal conversion if he attends a Jewish school and follows a course of studies leading to Confirmation." The Task Force understands that the questions of matrilineal-patrilineal descent are being presently reviewed by the CCAR to determine whether there should be any further changes. The Task Force recognizes that this is a matter for determination by the Rabbis. However, the Task Force (more than one-third of whom are themselves rabbis) believes that it would be helpful for the CCAR to have the benefit of knowing the views of the members of the Task Force who have devoted considerable study and discussion concerning this issue. The Task Force believes that the realities of contemporary Jewish life as well as the highest ideals of Judaism require that any and all discriminatory references to either matrilineal or patrilineal descent be stricken from Reform Jewish practice and that in cases of doubt, the doubt should be resolved in favor of broadening the definition of who is deemed a Jew. This is all the more important in light of the decimation of our ranks brought about by the horror of the Holocaust.

<u>Introduction to Judaism Classes and Conversion Study Programs</u>

The Task Force believes that there is a great need for strengthening and improving Introduction to Judaism classes and overall conversion programs for people who may be interested in learning more about Judaism or who may be or are considering conversion to Judaism. Within this frame of reference, the Task Force recommends the adoption of the following Resolution:

3.   The Task Force on Reform Jewish Outreach has found that
there are an increasing number of people who seek information about Judaism and the Jewish people, including individuals
considering conversion to Judaism. To help meet the needs
of these people, the Task Force believes it is important
that there be strengthening and improvement of Introduction
to Judaism classes and overall conversion programs. In part,
this involves better communication among congregations, many
of whom already have excellent programs but could benefit from
an exchange of information from other congregations across the
country. There is also a need for additional materials in this
area (1) to have available for people who are involved in
Introduction to Judaism classes and/or the conversion process
already, and (2) for people who are undertaking study to learn
more about Judaism, including those who may be considering
the possibility of conversion.

> Follow-Through Programs for People Who Have Recently
> Chosen Judaism

The Task Force believes that there is a great need for inaugurating and improving "follow-through" programs for people who have
recently chosen Judaism. Within this frame of reference, the Task
Force urges the adoption of the following Resolution:

4.   The Task Force On Reform Jewish Outreach believes there
is a great need for better "follow-through" programs for
people who have recently chosen Judaism as their religion.
This involves both single persons and married persons and
their families. Our Task Force Study has shown that there
are unique problems that those who come to Judaism face,
ranging from the need for full acceptance and participation
in the synagogue and general Jewish community to the need
for sensitivity to the relationships of these people with
their non-Jewish family and friends. We must be more
sensitive to these problems and there should be literature
and programs developed to help meet the special needs of
those individuals.

Reform Jewish Outreach to Persons of No Religious Preference

The Task Force has concluded that seeking converts is entirely within the historic traditions of Judaism. The Task Force believes that any program of Reform Jewish Outreach should primarily involve communicating with dignity the message of Judaism to unaffiliated Jews (including those born of mixed marriages) and to non-Jews who have no religious preference - a message that explains the values, history and traditions of Judaism and the Jewish people and that emphasizes the rich, warm and open tradition of our faith and the uniqueness of Judaism and, most importantly, lets people know that Judaism is not a closed society, but welcomes those who wish to enter its ranks.

The Task Force has concluded that there are important collateral benefits that can arise from an informational Outreach program of this kind. For instance, a sensitively prepared informational program about Judaism would be heard by all Americans, including unaffiliated Jews who may be inspired to return to a more active identification with Judaism. It would also be heard by other Americans who may have no desire to consider choosing Judaism as their religion but nevertheless would gain an understanding about Judaism that would help dispel myth and suspicion.

Such an undertaking, if done properly, will have great impact upon born Jews, particularly those who are ambivalent about their own Jewishness. Jewish college students, so often assailed by missionaries and representatives of cults and charismatic movements, will learn that Judaism is a faith that attracts countless young people like themselves who have found fulfillment in its practices. Higher rates of synagogue affiliation, greater interest in books of Jewish content and more positive Jewish identification may well be collateral benefits accruing from this project.

There are other collateral benefits that can be achieved, including the benefits that one receives as a teacher when one is imparting education about a religion to another person.

The Task Force, therefore, recommends the adoption of the following Resolution:

5.   The Task Force On Reform Jewish Outreach recommends that Reform Judaism communicate to the general public information about the history, traditions, beliefs and values of Judaism - that Judaism is a loving, meaningful, spiritual religion that welcomes all who wish to embrace it. However, the Task Force does not believe that Reform Judaism should have programs of Outreach directed toward adherents of other religions.

To create and implement positive programs of communication about Judaism to the general public, the Task Force recommends that the Reform movement consult with the most qualified experts, including those in the field of communications, to assist in research, planning, producing and disseminating program ideas and programs, as well as preparing literature, audio-visual, and other educational materials.

Because most of the publicity in the general news media about the work of the Task Force has concentrated on the question of whether or not there should be a Reform Jewish Outreach program to the millions of Americans of no religious preference, the Task Force believes it is appropriate to add some additional background in this portion of its Report.

When Rabbi Schindler in December, 1978, proposed that Reform Jews consider adopting an Outreach program "aimed at all Americans who are unchurched and who are seeking roots in religion", there was wide discussion among both Jews and non-Jews. Some rabbis and lay persons expressed concern that Christians might "retaliate" by actively seeking converts among Jewish young people. However, according to a survey conducted by Rabbi Balfour Brickner who was then the Director of the UAHC/CCAR Commission on Interreligious Affairs, leading Catholic and Protestant theologians generally supported the proposals of Rabbi Schindler.

"An active Judaism which vigorously proclaims its own unique message to the world and openly invites all interested in experiencing the richness and depth of its religious tradition is something to be welcomed in a pluralistic society," said Dr. Eugene Fisher of the National Conference of Catholic Bishops.

Peter Berger, a Protestant associated with the Mediating Structures Project in New York City, stated: "Judaism will convince 'its own' only if it succeeds in convincing others. . . . A religious community in a pluralistic society will increasingly find that it will be plausible to those within it only if it can make itself plausible to outsiders."

Many Christian leaders agreed with Dr. Berger's thesis that an Outreach program would strengthen self-understanding and identification among members of the Jewish community. Others praised Rabbi Schindler's call as demonstrating the vitality of Judaism and the Jewish community in this country.

The terms "missionizing" or even "proselytizing" are incorrect and inapplicable for what the Task Force recommends as a program of Reform Jewish Outreach. In a pluralistic society, where Jews are woven into the fabric of American life and culture at levels unparalleled in history, there is an obvious need for a thoughtfully prepared, coordinated program of information that explains Judaism and Jewish history to the entire public - Jews and non-Jews alike - and lets Jews and non-Jews know that the Jewish religion is open to all. This is the definition of "Outreach" as designated by the Task Force on Reform Judaism.

The Task Force agrees that any Jewish Outreach program should distinguish itself from the evangelical efforts of others who seek to convert people to their own religion, even though those people might already identify with another religion. Any program of Reform Jewish Outreach should in no way seek to convert to Judaism people who identify with other religions. However, the Task Force has determined that there is need for research into the special concerns of the religiously nonpreferenced. There is a tremendous potential for rendering an invaluable service to countless men and women yearning for a religious focus for themselves and their children and who might want to consider Judaism as one of the possibilities.

Hopes that the declining Jewish population will be arrested by the swelling of Jewish ranks through conversion should not be rejected as inconsequential or irrelevant. Such prospects should be placed in proper perspective, however. A Program of Outreach undertaken solely as a means of compensating for the limited birth rate among Jews is no rationale for its implementation. Nor are the arguments of those of its opponents who, in pointing to the special character of the Jewish people and historic role of the "saving remnant," would abandon the project solely because we have always been a small group who take upon ourselves special duties and responsibilities.

There is no doubt that efforts to intensify Jewish awareness and Jewish practice should take place. But it is fallacious to argue that we must first "put our own house in order." If anything, both projects - Outreach to unaffiliated Jews and to unaffiliated non-Jews - are linked inextricably, one to another, and each can only benefit from the other.

Finally, the Task Force has concluded that there is a great need for more books, pamphlets, films and other educational materials that explain the uniqueness of Judaism and what Judaism has to offer and particularly what Reform Judaism has to offer to the individual and to society. These materials can be of great help in meeting the needs of the non-Jewish partner in a mixed marriage, the children of mixed marriages, those people who have already decided to seek conversion to Judaism, and those people who have recently converted to Judaism. The preparation of these materials and the financing of the cost of publication and distribution is a matter that should be given high priority. We also recommend that those developing materials for an Outreach program should work closely with the UAHC/CCAR Commission on Jewish Education.

In addition to the adoption of the foregoing Resolutions, the Task Force adopted the following formal statement concerning the question, "Should the Task Force explore at this time the issue of whether Rabbis should officiate at mixed-marriage cere-monies":

"During the course of the Task Force study, a number of people asked if the Task Force would involve itself with the issue of whether rabbis should officiate at mixed-marriages. This is a soul-searching question with strong opinions on both sides. However, after much thought and discussion, the Task Force determined that it would not attempt to deal with this issue in the context of its 1981 Report. Instead, the Task Force decided to concentrate its efforts in the five primary areas that are encompassed in the formal Resolutions that have been adopted for presentation to the 1981 Biennial. The Joint UAHC/CCAR Task Force in its continuing study after the 1981 Biennial will include on its agenda the exploration of this issue."

In adopting the foregoing formal statement, the Task Force found that its members had a wide diversity of backgrounds and opinions. Nevertheless, as in the case of the adoption of the five Resolutions, the decision of the Task Force was unanimous.

In its deliberations, the Task Force recognized that to some degree Reform Judaism has already undertaken a program of Outreach. The very fact that substantial numbers of people who have not been born Jewish have chosen to identify as Jews, to marry as Jews, and to raise their children as Jews, is of great significance. What the Task Force has recommended is to take the next step forward in the five specific areas of our inquiry.

The Task Force has determined that the implementation of a program of Reform Jewish Outreach will enhance that which is already an intrinsic part of the fabric of American Jewish life and will also contribute to the betterment of America. However, in order to realize the tremendous potential of this program, we will need the support and encouragement of our rabbis and congregational leadership.

We believe that we are engaged in a sacred task, and that in extolling the virtues of Judaism to others, we testify to its significance in our own lives. We stand convinced that a positive program of Outreach to the religiously non-preferenced, implemented in accordance with the limitations and provisions already mentioned, is in the best interest of our country and also represents yet another step in the restoration of the authentic Jewish self and the reconsecration of the Jewish people as an eternal people and as a people of God.

CONCLUSION

The members of the Task Force are indebted to Rabbi Alexander Schindler for his visionary genius in calling for the organization of our Task Force to study the many facets of a Reform Jewish Outreach program - a study which could result in one of the great milestones in American Jewish history - and, indeed, in world Jewish history. And we are also indebted to the Board of Trustees of the Union of American Hebrew Congregations and the Central Conference of American Rabbis for having the wisdom and courage to join together in this important undertaking.

We members of the Task Force came from a wide variety of backgrounds and experiences and initially had many differing points of view. Yet, we were able to arrive at a unanimous agreement that there should be programs of Reform Jewish Outreach.

Within the frame of reference of this Report, the Task Force recommends Reform Jewish Outreach programs to meet the needs of the non-Jewish partner in a mixed marriage, children of mixed marriages, people who have already decided to seek conversion to Judaism and persons who have recently converted to Judaism. We also agreed that there should be a dignified program of Reform Jewish Outreach to persons of no religious preference, which would involve communication of information to the general public about the history, traditions, beliefs, and values of Judaism - that Judaism is a loving, meaningful, spiritual religion that welcomes all who wish to embrace it. However, the Task Force does not believe that Reform Judaism should have programs of Outreach directed toward adherents of other religions.

The Task Force believes that an Outreach program undertaken in accordance with the limitations and provisions discussed in the Task Force Report will have many collateral benefits for both affiliated and unaffiliated Jews (including those born of mixed marriages) and will also enhance the life of America in general and American Jewish life in particular.

In the concluding portion of the letter accompanying the distribution of this Report to the member congregations of the UAHC, Chairman David Belin has written:

"We do not expect that every person will agree with all of our findings and recommendations. But we hope everyone will recognize that we undertook our work in an atmosphere of full and frank discussion in the greatest tradition of our faith.

"Truly, we are at one of the major crossroads in the history of the Jews. The direction that we take will have a tremendous impact on our future and on the future of our country."

For us, it has been both an opportunity and a privilege to participate in this historical study that we hope will play a major role in insuring the continuance of a healthy, vital American Jewish community - a goal that will benefit the Jewish people and, equally important, benefit all of the people of our country and, indeed, people throughout the world. The contributions of the Jewish people to humankind have been many. Let us fervently hope and pray that these contributions continue in the centuries ahead.

I.   INTRODUCTION

     Note to Facilitators: During the course of the group
you will probably be asked many questions directly by
group members, since an important aspect of this group
is informational and you are perceived to be the resident "expert". In order not to be trapped into feeling
put on the spot and offering apparently instant solutions, we suggest that you consider the following when
a direct question is asked of you:

     1) Before answering, open the question up to the
     group. Asking "What do others think about Susan's
     questions?", "Does anyone have any ideas about
     this?" "John and Ellen, you talked about similar
     concerns last week. Have you had any further
     thoughts that might be useful to Susan?" will pro-
     mote group process and facilitate a full discussion
     of the issue raised.

     2) Be sensitive to how the question is asked. If
     the person seems distressed, don't be afraid to
     acknowledge it. Examples: "Mary, you seem to have
     some pretty strong feelings about these issues...."
     or "This seems to be a painful topic for everyone."
     Commenting on feelings will provide participants
     with the opportunity to talk about Judaism and their
     relationship with an awareness of their own emotion-
     al process.

     3) Don't be afraid to acknowledge that you don't
     have all the answers, and that there are many
     aspects of relationships that aren't always pre-
     dictable.

     4) You may notice that your answers to some of
     these questions will change from group to group, or
     even according to the particular individual within
     the group who has asked the question. Many of
     these responses are highly subjective, and your own
     thinking will probably change somewhat over time.

II.   MY PARTNER AND ME

WILL LOVE ENDURE WITH THE DIFFERENCE IN OUR BACKGROUND?

     "Part of the difficulty of making any long-term
commitment to another person is that relationships come
with no guarantees! Differences in background often
mean that couples have to develop special sensitivities
and deal with complex issues. I think it's important

to acknowledge that all of you in this group just by deciding to participate in this group have taken the first step toward a deeper understanding of one another and are starting on the right foot.

WHAT COMPROMISES SHOULD WE MAKE? SHOULD WE AGREE TO GIVE "EQUAL TIME" TO EACH OTHER'S RELIGIOUS BELIEFS?

"Through our Outreach efforts over the past few years (which we have discussed in other sessions), we have learned to help couples look at those very issues. Since every couple is different there just aren't any magic solutions. You probably noted that even within this group there are some striking differences in the ways that you approach issues we have discussed." OR: "You have probably noticed that I've said very little about working out the logistics of his and her religions in the home. That's because in my experience, that plan doesn't seem to work very well. It is difficult when dealing with issues such as these to define parameters which guarantee "equal time" and pat solutions. In addition, what may seem to be an acceptable arrangement for both partners now becomes unmanageable when there are children. Can you imagine a child going to Shabbat services on Friday night, Jewish religious school some Sundays and Christian Sunday school on alternate weeks, and Hebrew School on Tuesday afternoon? The poor kid will be confused and exhausted!"

HOW CAN I EDUCATE MY SPOUSE ABOUT TRADITIONS AND HOLIDAYS IN A NON-THREATENING WAY?

"Let's start by asking the group. You're all spouses (or spouses to be) and you all probably have the same question. What do you think? Let's talk about that word 'threatening' for a minute. What does that mean? What would be threatening to you personally? I think the formula is really simple: From my perspective you might begin by discussing any religious activity beforehand with your partner. Would he or she like to participate? In what way? What could you do to make that experience as comfortable as possible? It may be a matter of sharing some information before the event. Or, just as important, it may mean simply that you let him or her know that you understand that there may be some discomfort and awkwardness. This doesn't always need to be articulated verbally -- sometimes a hand squeeze will do."

III.   <u>RELIGIOUS IDENTITY AND MARRIAGE</u>

HOW CAN I HAVE MY RELIGION WITHOUT STIFLING HIS OR HERS?

"I have to say honestly that I don't know the answer. I'm not sure this is possible. What do you think?" <u>OR</u> "We seem to be back on this theme of his and hers religions again. Suppose my answer to your question was a simple 'No.' Where would we go in our discussion from here?"

HOW CAN WE PRACTICE OUR SEPARATE FAITHS AND STILL HAVE A UNIFIED HOME?

"Mary, I'm touched by your determination to solve potential problems early so that they don't become stumbling blocks in your relationship later on. We have been talking about this for two weeks now, and so far no one has been able to come up with an answer. To talk about 'separate faiths' and 'unity' seems like a contradiction in terms. Perhaps the answer lies in the word 'home'. Do you think that there is a way that you could agree to have one religion in the home, thereby making it unified? Let's talk about that idea to see if it helps us begin to get a handle on this..."

HOW DO I DEAL WITH MY FEELINGS ABOUT GIVING UP PART OF MY IDENTITY AND HERITAGE?

(<u>Note to facilitator</u>: Clarify what "giving up" means. Has this issue been discussed in the group? What is to be given up? etc.)

"What are your feelings right now as you're asking this question? Then: "How do you imagine you'll feel in the future?" "I was pleased to see last week how critically the group was examining religious commitment on both sides. I wonder if that discussion put you in touch with aspects of your religious identity which you hadn't thought about for awhile..." "Are you going to have deal with those painful feelings all by yourself? Who could help you?"

CAN MY NON-JEWISH SPOUSE EVER APPRECIATE MY JEWISH IDENTITY?

"Absolutely! Your Jewish identity is a part of what he or she fell in love with, even though neither of you realize it. Fuller understanding is something that will happen over time, with exposure to some of the kinds of experiences that shaped your Jewish identity: holidays, life cycle events, and involvement with a Jewish family. It's a wonderful opportunity for you to be his or her teacher." <u>OR</u>: "I'm not sure what you're asking, Mark. Are there parts of your Jewish identity that Helen doesn't understand?" (What are they? Refocus the group discussion.) "It's often hard for non-Jews to understand why Judaism is so important to us when we may go to synagogue only rarely. We seem to have automatic antennae for anti-semitism and we seem to be concerned about intermarriage. It doesn't make a lot of sense on the surface. But usually such issues can be explained very simply through a combination of frank discussion, education, and encounters with Jews and Judaism. All of which we're doing here! Aren't you glad you came?!"

HOW MAY WE, AS A COUPLE (CHRISTIAN AND JEWISH), PRESERVE THE BEST OF OUR INDIVIDUAL RELIGIONS AND STILL RAISE A JEWISH CHILD IN A HARMONIOUS WAY?

"When a choice is made for the religious identity of a child in an intermarriage, there is always fear of disharmony. However, the parents have already taken a positive step in dealing with these feelings by choosing to give the child a religious identity - in this case, Judaism. In honoring this commitment, parents not only preserve the best of Judaism, but, at the same time, enable the child to learn about and respect the best of the Christian family's religion without its taking away from a Jewish identity. Such clarification of the differences present in an intermarriage prevents the denigration of either religion by reducing their traditions to mere superficial celebrations by everyone.

WHAT MAY BE THE LONG TERM EFFECTS ON OUR MARRIAGE?

"I don't know. Statistics about the long term success of intermarriages are not yet available. What are you particularly concerned about?" Then: "What do you think could be done to prevent any negative effect on your marriage?

HOW CAN A PARTNER MAINTAIN HIS OR HER OWN RELIGIOUS IDENTITY IF IT IS NOT THE DOMINANT RELIGION OF THE HOUSEHOLD?

"That's a good question. First of all, if there is a strong commitment on the part of that partner, it can be done successfully. It's important to remember that although your primary focus is on each other right now, your families and friends hopefully will remain important parts of your lives. Holiday celebrations and religious experience can be shared with parents, other relatives, or friends. Let me give you an example:

There is no reason why an intermarried couple who has agreed to have Jewish home can't go with their children to Grandma Maureen's for Christmas. I think it's important to underline that we will always have families, memories, and some very strong emotional ties to our pasts.

SO WON'T ANY AGREEMENTS WE MAKE NOW BE USELESS SINCE OUR FEELINGS WILL CHANGE ANYWAY?

"There is something that is much more important than any decision you make now: the process of learning to discuss these issues in a way that is healthy and productive for your relationship. Much of what you have been doing in this group has been learning how to talk about religion with each other and with your families. Those are invaluable skills that will stay with you to help keep the lines of communication open every step of the way. You'll have the basic skills you need to deal with changes as they arise."

HOW IMPORTANT REALLY IS ALL THE OUTER STUFF ABOUT RELIGION? WHAT ABOUT THE REAL SPIRITUAL LOVING CONNECTION WE HAVE? AM I MAKING A BIG DEAL ABOUT NOTHING?

"Of course, the loving bond that you have with your partner is important, whether it is defined in spiritual terms or not. It is the basic ingredient of a good, healthy relationship. The importance of the 'outer stuff about religion' is what you need to determine for yourself. You must feel it has some importance or you wouldn't be here. This really is the topic of some of the early sessions of the program: what does it mean to me to be Jewish/Christian? To those who care deeply about and are committed to their religion, religious identity is not 'outer stuff'."

IV.   PARENTS AND FAMILY

HOW CAN I DEAL WITH MY PARENT'S DISCOMFORT WITH CHANGING EXPECTATIONS FOR ME? SPECIFICALLY, HOW CAN I HANDLE THEIR DISAPPOINTMENT, EVEN ANGER?

"It is important to place this discussion in the context of the normal process of separation between parents and children that occurs with a marriage. How would your parents respond if you married a Jew with little education, or one who was too 'unacceptable' to them in some way, etc. (Is anyone good enough for their baby?) Some of these feelings may be hung on the

convenient peg of intermarriage. Some parents may go
through a mourning period as they give up their personal dream of your future. The process of separation takes time for them as for you; it does not
happen all at once during the wedding ceremony. Understanding, reassurance of your love for them and time
all help this process along." (It might be helpful to
role-play a parent-child discussion so that group members can model for each other.)

WILL MY SPOUSE'S PARENTS ACCEPT JEWISH GRANDCHILDREN?

"There is, of course, no clearcut response to this
question. People are different and respond to the situations they are presented with in different ways.
Grandmother and grandfather may respond in different
ways. There may be a religious issue involved, such as
fundamentalist Christian grandparents fearing their
grandchild will not be saved. On the other hand, this
is often an interpersonal issue. A parent may fear
that   the grandchild will be different in some way,
will not love him or her as fully, or the parents may
feel betrayed. Many parents need some time to adjust
to changed expectations and to experience the love that
can grow between them and their grandchildren. Perhaps
the best indicator of your in-laws' response to having
Jewish grandchildren will be their response to other
challenges in the past."

I HAVE TROUBLE DEALING WITH THE FACT THAT EVERYONE
(IN-LAWS, MY PARENTS, FIANCE) CANNOT BE HAPPY WITH THE
ULTIMATE DECISIONS? HOW DO OTHERS DEAL WITH THIS?

(To the facilitator: This is a good topic for discussion. Points for the facilitator to bear in mind:
the maturity of each participant will influence his
or her response to this question, a more mature person
feeling that personal integrity would carry more weight
in decision-making than the happiness of others; how
do you define "happiness?" It might be more useful to
talk about levels of acceptance and the individual's
comfort in living with a higher or lower level of
parental acceptance; whose happiness is most important
to you--yours, your partner's, your parents, your in-
laws? This question demonstrates one of the additional
issues to be dealt with by engaged rather than married
couples.)

I WOULD LIKE TO DISCUSS HOW PARTICIPANT'S PARENTS
HAVE REACTED TO THEIR SITUATIONS AND HOW IMPORTANT OR
UNIMPORTANT DEALING WITH THIS REACTION IS IN THE
ULTIMATE DECISIONS THEY MAKE.

(To the facilitator: It might be useful to include

Sherri's Herb and Mary Kushner scenario here to focus attention on the paralyzing effect of opposite pulls from two sets of parents. See Appendix 12.)

"The couples themselves must make the ultimate decisions for their family and they must be able to live with the consequent feelings of their parents. What is meant by 'ultimate decisions?' This most likely refers to decisions relating to childrearing. It might be important to note at some point that, as important as it is to make decisions of childrearing, such decisions are not written in stone. They can be changed if they become unworkable. Changing the idea of 'ultimate decisions' to the idea of the process of decision making may alleviate some of the anxiety surrounding these issues."

V.   CHILDREN

DO PEOPLE'S RELIGIOUS VIEWS BECOME STRONGER ONCE THEY ARE MARRIED AND HAVE CHILDREN?

"Yes, in our experience, they often do become stronger. Religion isn't static; it changes in relation to changes we experience throughout our lives. You probably don't feel the same way now about your religion as you did as a child. Many of us don't realize this, and we are caught off guard by the intensity of religious feelings raised by the birth of a child, for instance, when we never felt those feelings before."

IF YOU ARE A JEW AND YOUR SPOUSE ISN'T AND EACH ACCEPTS THE OTHER'S RELIGION, THEN HOW DO YOU DECIDE WHICH RELIGION TO CHOOSE FOR YOUR CHILDREN?

IF YOU CHOOSE TO RAISE YOUR CHILDREN AS JEWS, HOW DO YOU EXPLAIN TO THEM THAT THEIR MOTHER/FATHER BELONGS TO A DIFFERENT FAITH?

"Children in an intermarriage will have a religious identity if parents agree to make a choice - a decision made difficult when the parents themselves come from two different religious backgrounds.

In order to do so, partners must first be willing to explore in depth what their own religious identities mean to them and what each believes is important in nurturing someone else's religious identity. With this honest evaluation, parents can begin to explain to children why a choice is necessary, why one parent feels the need to remain who he or she is and thus provide a basis for sensitivity to the parent whose religion was not chosen."

IF YOU DECIDE TO RAISE YOUR CHILDREN ACCORDING TO YOUR SPOUSE'S RELIGION:

    A.   HOW DO YOU DEAL WITH YOUR FEELINGS?

    B.   HOW DO YOU RECONCILE NOT BEING ABLE TO PRACTICE YOUR RELIGION WITH YOUR CHILDREN?

    C.   HOW DO YOU PREVENT YOURSELF FROM BECOMING AN OUTSIDER TO YOUR CHILDREN AND YOUR SPOUSE?

"If one spouse decides to raise the children in the other spouse's religion, it is crucial that feelings are dealt with openly and honestly on an on-going basis, understand that feelings change in response to life experiences and situations. By keeping in touch with how you feel and communicating those feelings with a loving spouse and family, you enable others to be sensitive to you and to respond to your needs in a supportive way.

You can reconcile your choice to honor a commitment to raise children in a religion different than your own by being respected and supported in your decision to practice your religion privately in a way that you feel comfortable.

If you are free to express who you are in a way that does not undermine your commitment to your children, you can return that respect by helping your children celebrate who they are in the context of a supportive family united by a shared commitment."

HOW DOES ONE INSTILL JEWISH IDENTITY, VALUES, HISTORY IN CHILDREN WHILE MAINTAINING A FAMILY UNIT WHICH DOES EXCLUDE THE NON-JEWISH PARTNER?

"When two religions are practiced in the home, and the choice has been made to raise Jewish children, it is still possible to maintain a family unit without excluding the non-Jewish partner as long as each spouse is respectful and sensitive to the needs of the other.

The non-Jewish partner must be willing to honor a Jewish commitment for the children by learning what is important in shaping a Jewish identity for the children and subsequently participating in the process of education and celebration needed to fulfill that goal.

Similarly, the Jewish partner must be willing to respect and support the non-Jewish spouse's religious choice; the children should be taught to respect this choice. Great sensitivity must be exercised by the Jewish family members to include and encourage participation by the non-Jewish spouse and to recognize feelings of loss and pain that the non-Jew may experience at different times throughout the relationship as a result of having a separate religious identity."

IS IT POSSIBLE TO RAISE CHILDREN WITH TWO RELIGIONS:

"Children need and want to feel belongingness, an identity as a member of a family, group, or community. They ask questions of 'who am I' and form that identity by taking clues from their parents and peers.

In the process of developing an identity, children use parents as role models and are concerned first about being like 'Mommy' and 'Daddy', and then later search for an identity as a belonging member of a group or community.

In our American pluralistic society, religions are often seen as variations of a common religious theme, yet, by definition they represent very different commitments and understanding of fundamental truths.

Thus, although children may learn from each parent what his or her religion means and represents for him or her, unless a choice is made, the children cannot become full members of either religion - an essential part of forming one's own identity."

IS IT A PROBLEM FOR CHILDREN TO HAVE PARENTS PRACTICING TWO DIFFERENT RELIGIONS IN THE HOUSEHOLD?

"Although an underlying awareness of difference exists when parents practice two religions in the home, a problem for children would manifest itself only if both parents were not comfortable with that possibility and were thus incapable of communicating truthfully with children about these very differences.

It would be important for parents to make a choice for the children's religious identity and subsequently work out a way of being sensitive and supportive of the parent whose religious identity was not chosen.

This would deal with feelings of loss and lessen any jealousy or competition that would undermine a desire for mutual respect rather than blur the differences present in the home.

Such a decision could then be communicated with other family members and friends in such a way as to elicit understanding and support to pave the way for relationships sensitive to the unique situation of the practice to two religions in the home.

VI.   COMMUNITY AND ACCEPTANCE

HOW WILL WE BE VIEWED BY THE COMMUNITY AT LARGE?

"In North America today there are many intermarried families and many communities in which to live. People with prejudicial attitudes may be found anywhere; most intermarried families have nevertheless found a comfortable community for themselves. A local Reform congregation may be a good place to start."

HOW CAN I AS A JEWISH PARTNER IN AN INTERMARRIAGE BE PART OF THE JEWISH COMMUNITY?

"Jewish partners in intermarriage are accepted in Reform congregations with no restrictions at all. Some Conservative and Orthodox congregations might place certain restrictions on ritual participation or leadership positions for an intermarried Jew. Although you may encounter individuals in communal organizations who have negative attitudes toward intermarriage, you will generally be welcomed warmly as someone willing to work toward organizational goals."

WILL MY SPOUSE, A CHRISTIAN, BE ACCEPTED WITHOUT CONVERSION IN A SYNAGOGUE, IF WE AS A FAMILY DECIDE TO JOIN AS A FAMILY RAISING A JEWISH CHILD?

"Your spouse will be accepted in all reform congregations. He or she will be welcome to participate in worship services and in many other aspects of temple life - choir, adult education, temple committees, etc. It is important to ask at the temple you are considering joining about their particular membership policy. Many temples do not permit non-Jews to hold leadership positions in the congregation or to participate on the bimah in certain rituals. In general, however, non-Jewish family members are welcomed and their participation is encouraged."

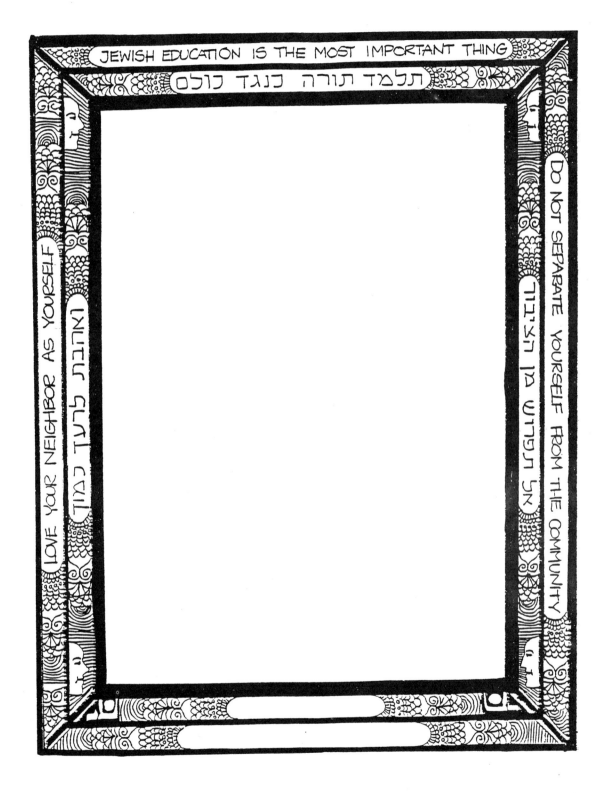

Marriage of Christians and Jews

Ronald Osborne

Judaism and Christianity live and interact asymmetrically, and this is the cause of much of the difficulty Jews and Christians experience when they marry.

Osborne, Ronald. "Marriage of Christians and Jews." Plumbline. Volume 13, Issue 3. September 1985.

Reprinted with permission of author.

Jewish-Christian dialogue has yielded increased understanding and a greater sense of respect and mutuality between Christians and Jews, but it has not yet ameliorated the pain and conflict experienced by Jews and Christians when they marry each other, or try to stay married to each other, or indeed find that they cannot remain married.

I want to attempt to clarify some of these problems. My purpose is not to encourage or discourage Jews and Christians in marrying each other. It is to share some observations which may help name at least some of the problems so that, knowing their names, these problems might be managed.

My data come from several sources: from pastoral experience in guiding preparation for marriage by such persons, from marriage counseling, and from many conversations over the years with both Jewish and Christian colleagues and friends.

* * *

Judaism and Christianity live and interact asymmetrically. This fact is obscured by American religious pluralism which tends to regard all religions as variations on a common religious theme. I suggest this asymmetry is the cause of much of the difficulty Jews and Christians experience when they marry.

The theological dimensions of the asymmetry can be seen in the instance of worship. When Christians worship with Jews there is almost nothing they cannot affirm. They can participate fully without reservation in the liturgical life of the synagogue, Holy Day rituals, even family rituals. There is hardly anything which is religiously inaccessible to them, at least in theological terms. There may be cultural barriers. Some Jews may prefer not to have at least some Christians around in their synagogues or in their homes, and some Christians feel uncomfortable with some Jews. But the theological content of Judaism is not an offense or stumbling black (a *"scandelon"* as the New Testament calls it) to Christians. To be sure, Christians would want to say much more than what is said in Jewish affirmations, but they can *at least* say what Jews do.

The obverse is not the case. Christianity is not

The Rev. Ronald Osborne is chaplain at the University of Iowa, Iowa City, Iowa.

What does a couple do about on-going relationships to church and synagogue and family?

equally accessible to Jews. When Jews worship with Christians almost nothing is accessible, almost everything is problematic. "Old Testament" (even to call it that already denies Jewish understandings, since there is to the Jewish mind but one testament always old but ever made new) readings are selected in the Christian lectionaries to interpret New Testament experience. Even the Psalms gather Christian meanings. It is not enough to advise Jews to participate only in the Jewish parts of the Christian liturgy, because the "Jewish" content of Christian liturgy has a *publically* Christian meaning; thus, to participate at all might mean giving assent to these public meanings. Of course, the distinctively "Christian" content of Christian worship, "New Testament" readings, creeds, prayers, trinitarian invocations, acclamations and doxologies, are all utterly impossible to a Jewish participant, or at least to one with theological sensitivity and integrity.

This, of course, is not to say that Jews do not find ways to participate in Christian worship in ways they find comfortable. Sometimes just being present while not participating very directly in the worship service is a Jewish way of indicating support and affirmation of Christian colleagues and friends without claiming commonalities which do not exist.

One can state the asymmetry of worship abstractly, by simply noting that much Jewish theological content can be affirmed by Christians, very much less Christian theological content can be affirmed by a Jew. This can be put more strongly. Christians have persecuted Jews for not affirming more, and Jewish tradition has almost nothing positive to say about Christianity. It largely ignores it.

This asymmetry makes the planning of a marriage rite for Jews and Christians extremely problematic, and it complicates subsequent relationships enormously. What does a couple do about on-going relationships to church and synagogue and family? How are children reared religiously? How are important family events to be celebrated? What is the religious commonality in the marital relationship itself? What symbols interpret the relationship, give it meaning and depth, provide resources for hard times, celebrate the good? How is the relationship to be anchored in a ground of meaning which has tradition and community?

* * *

A second kind of asymmetry is cultural. While both Christianity and Judaism are lived through cultural forms, the relationship of faith to ethnicity is different for each. Each faith tends to misinterpret the other because of the difference.

Judaism is both an ethnic and religious phenomenon. In this century the ethnic and religious dimensions of Jewishness have been separated. Large numbers of Jews think of themselves as Jews and are thought of as Jews even though they have no palpable religious commitment. On the other hand, almost all persons who affirm Jewish religious beliefs and belong to Jewish religious communities of some kind are ethnically Jewish. Proselytes seem to adopt Jewish ethnicity quickly.

For Christians, at least in theological terms, there is no such thing as a Christian ethnicity. One is not a Christian because one's mother is, as is the case in Judaism. One is a Christian because one has been baptized and seeks to live out the meaning of the baptismal covenant.

Judaism survives and continues because of family relationships. The religion rides the back of ethnicity. Christianity survives and continues because each generation claims anew the Gospel.

Having said this it must be conceded that these theological distinctions may not seem very apparent in everyday life. A friend tells of attending a high school in an eastern city in which there were two ethnic groups, Italian Catholics and Jews. The two groups entered the building by separate entrances, took separate courses to the extent possible and maintained separate extracurricular programs. The Italians controlled sports, the Jews dominated debate and the chess and science clubs. To this person the relationship between religion and ethnicity seemed the same for each of these groups.

Another friend tells of living in a Jewish neighborhood in an eastern city adjacent to a Polish neighborhood. Both attended the same schools except that the Polish children who attended public schools were mostly children who had been expelled from the parochial schools. To this person the relationship of religion to ethnicity seemed the same except that Christians were perceived as persons with severe learning and behavior problems! Because Jews come largely from urban areas where ethnic realities are important social facts, they probably have perceptions of the Christians which are colored strongly by the kinds of experiences noted above. They see the relationship of ethnicity to religion to be the same for others as for themselves.

Christians are less likely to have comparable perceptions, except, of course, for those groups in which ethnicity remains very strong. Christians are more inclined to see Judaism simply as another religious denomination, one of many voluntary religious communities.

The rub comes when Jewish and Christian teenagers leave home for college. Often enough, a Jewish youth who has only known Christians in ethnic terms meets a Christian youth who has only known of Jews second-hand through novels, and they fall in love. Each must struggle mightily to look beyond the culturally-given experiences they have had to understand the meaning of the other's identity.

I have had personal knowledge of relationships in which the Jewish partner is not religiously Jewish, but who nevertheless insists the children not be reared as Christians. One can understand the Jewish perspective. If Jewishness is largely cultural and there is a certain disenchantment with religion, or a secularization of religious belief, and if one cannot hope that much of the cultural Jewishness can be passed on in one's own family, one can at least keep a religiousness which one finds obnoxious from being propagated in one's own house. This reasoning, insofar as it is reasoning, seems perverse to the Christian partner. Considerable resentment accrues. There is something terribly unfair about not caring enough about one's own religion to embrace it and practice it, while denying to one's offspring the religious heritage of one's spouse, it seems to the Christian.

I know no one — no one who cares about religious meaning anyway — who has found a satisfactory strategy for resolving this conflict. My impression is that Jewish-Christian couples in which both partners have strong religious commitments find acceptable ways to rear their children. But when one partner is not religious and the other is, there are almost no good options. The strategy often pursued is that of raising children with exposure to both religious traditions but without commitments to either. While this is something which could be profitably studied empirically, my unsystematic observations suggest that parents seldom find this satisfactory. It appears

that what happens is that the children are not exposed to either religious tradition sufficiently to feel religious meanings from the inside out. Since religion is caught, not taught, it is never caught. They, in fact, are raised as pagans.

* * *

There is also an asymmetrical way in which religious practice is institutionalized in Christianity and Judaism. For Jews the fundamental working entity for religious life is the family, which is where important religious celebrations happen. The synagogue, even though it has certain liturgical functions and has acquired meanings which once belonged only to the family, is fundamentally a school. The center of cultic life, the "priest figure" in Judaism, is in fact the Jewish Mother, although special roles are played by others, especially by elders. The Rabbi, an important person in the community, has very little cultic function. He is teacher and interpreter of the Torah, but less a priest than his own mother or wife.

For Christians the congregation in some form is the basic community entity. As important as family life is this larger family is the primary center for liturgical and cultic life. Even though this larger community may be organized in many different ways it remains a constant reality in Christian experience since the time the first believers "continued in the Apostles' teaching and fellowship and the prayers." The Rabbi, Priest, and Elder all become one person, the Bishop or the Priest who carries on all those functions. Other "ministers" have special representative roles, especially the Deacons, who extend the ministry of Christ's servanthood to the community and to the world. Family cultus, which is much less elaborate than in Jewish practice, is seen as supplemental to the liturgical life of the larger community, not the other way round. In fact, the Christian Eucharistic liturgy is the family Shabat meal of Jews with Christian meanings. Even the details of ceremonial are the same in some instances.

The equivalent institution to the Christian congregation or parish, therefore, is not the synagogue. It is the home.

A consequence of this institutional asymmetry is that when a Jew marries a Christian one of the basic constitutive elements of Jewish identity, the Jewish home, is destroyed. There is a sense in which every Jewish-Christian marriage is to Jews a kind of genocide. It is like closing a church and more. One church more or less doesn't matter

Judaism survives and continues because of family relationships...Christianity survives and continues because each generation claims anew the Gospel.

much to Christians. Churches are not propagated by family relationships. They are gathered by the grace of the Spirit and perhaps some organizing efforts. But to Jews each opportunity to establish a new Jewish family makes Jewish identity and survival less fragile. Most Jewish families, however open-minded, thus find a marriage outside the Jewish community extremely troubling.

There are therefore very few Rabbis willing to cooperate in arranging Jewish-Christian marriages. And there will continue to be some families who will consider a child dead who marries outside the community. In theological terms there is a sense in which such persons are dead. For a Jew to remove himself by marriage from Jewish family life is almost like a Christian refusing to attend Mass, or more like self excommunication. It is to cut oneself off from the supportive context for Jewish identity. There is a sense in which there is no such thing as an individual Jew. A Jew by definition is part of a people and the constituative institutions of that peoplehood are Jewish families.

Christians find these attitudes simply unfathomable. They seem like religious and ethnic chauvinism to them and represent a rigidity and intransigence they find irritating and grating. A Christian family does not give up the Christian identity of one of its members even when that member marries outside the faith. Christian identity can only be surrendered by an intentional act of apostasy. Christians cannot understand why Jews do not see things the same way.

* * *

A final point of radical divergence between Jewish and Christian perspective which colors all relationships including marriage relationships is divergent perceptions of the meaning of the holocaust. For Jews that event has an importance like that of the Exodus or the Exile. It is nearly impossible to be Jewish and not struggle somehow with the meaning of that event.

Most Christians who think about the holocaust at all see it not as an issue about which enormous personal struggle is necessary. It is but one instance of evil among many. To be sure, it is an instance of enormous proportions, but evil often has enormous proportions.

Jews often perceive Christian treatment of the holocaust in this way as a kind of anti-semitism. It does nothing, they think, to own up to the complicity they see of Christians in the holocaust, or in the cultural propensities for it laid down by

centuries of church-inspired hostility and persecution.

Christians, when confronted by these perceptions, are perplexed. The holocaust violates Christian values as much as Jewish. Jewish preoccupations with the event seem to represent a kind of ethnocentrism in the extreme. Is not any act of brutality an evil to be renounced? Why renounce only those evils which affect Jews? The implicit blame of the current generation of Christians by Jews requires an ethnic understanding of Christianity Christian theology cannot countenance.

All of this spills over into marriage relationships, and all other areas of conflict are intensified. The holocaust turns the asymmetry into cacophanous dissonance. There is probably no way Jews and Christians can marry without hearing that dissonance.

* * *

Young adults have enormous difficulty handling all of these things. What we know of ego development and of cognitive, moral, and religious development suggests that most young adults simply do not have the emotional and intellectual maturity to deal with these matters very well. They are struggling with the discovery of their own identities and often have to do that over and against the claims of family, whose concerns are often perceived as efforts to reduce independence and autonomy.

For many young adults religion itself is problematic. Many keep their distance as they move from tacit acquiescence to the religiousness of childhood and youth toward owning an explicit faith of their own. Many move toward that position by a protracted period of religious disinvolvement. Occasionally young adults interpret religious matters in terms of a naive universalism. Differences between religions are simplistically blurred so that there is the absence of an ability to make judgments about many of the critical questions to be resolved.

Often the marital relationship proposed is not seen as part of a larger social and religious context. It is a very private affair between two people. Family and religion are all resented as intrusive. What the couple wishes to celebrate is not the covenantal love of their respective religious traditions, neither Jewish "Hesed" nor Christian "Agape," but the erotic and philial love of American Romanticism.

I have deliberately painted a rather bleak picture here, partly to balance what I think are the naive concepts which abound platitudinously in our culture. The fact is that when Jews and Christians marry, people experience pain. That pain is real...

When Americans Intermarry

by Mark Winer

Only a generation ago intermarriage was a phenomenon on the fringe of American Jewish life. If my rabbi had asked us twenty-five years ago, few of my fellow Confirmands would have known any Jews married to non-Jews, certainly not in our own families. How much Jewish life has changed! Almost everyone has a close relative who has intermarried.

Recently I asked my Confirmation class if they knew anyone in their families married to a non-Jew. As we went around the room, only a couple of students could not cite a single incidence of intermarriage among their relatives. I myself could name half a dozen relatives married to non-Jews. Although the fringe phenomenon of intermarriage has not become the norm, it has certainly become commonplace within the past few decades.

Statistics on the frequency of Jewish intermarriage tell only part of the story, and like all statistics, they are subject to many interpretations. The most recent national survey is almost fifteen years old. According to the National Jewish Population Study, approximately one in three Jews entering marriage between 1965 and 1970 intermarried. Local community surveys completed more recently reveal such widely divergent rates that it is almost impossible to calculate the current Jewish intermarriage statistic based on their findings.

Even if the one in three rate has remained constant, what does it mean for the future of American Jewry? What does it reveal about Jewish education, the effectiveness of synagogues, and the strength of the Jewish family? Some rabbis, sociologists, and other commentators have viewed the intermarriage rate as evidence of a breakdown in American Jewish life. Many read the statistics as proof of our assimilation and predict a precipitous decline in the population of American Jewry. Numerous sermons and magazine articles bewail the "vanishing American Jew." While an earlier generation "sat shiva" for individual Jews who married non-Jews, many of this generation's Jewish leaders seem to be preparing for the death of American Jewry itself.

Dr. Mark Winer, senior rabbi of Temple Beth David, Commack NY, is also a sociologist who has conducted numerous studies on the American Jewish community.

Like all previous obituaries for the Jewish people, this death notice is premature. Careful examination of the statistics on Jewish intermarriage reveal a far more complex picture than originally perceived. While no one views intermarriage as healthy for the Jewish people, it need not be terminal. In the place of "shiva-sitting" and hand-wringing, Jewish leaders are evolving adaptive strategies to cope more effectively with the realities of intermarriage in the Jewish community. The UAHC Outreach effort and the CCAR's decision on patrilineal descent are among the most promising of these adaptive strategies.

Jewish parents are discovering that when one of their three children marries a non-Jew, it does not necessarily mean that he or she is rejecting them or Judaism. Sometimes the non-Jew converts to Judaism. Often the grandchildren are reared as Jews, attend religious school, and attain Bar/Bat Mitzvah and Confirmation—even if the non-Jewish parent never converts to Judaism. Temples

> "Jewish parents are discovering that when one of their three children marries a non-Jew, it does not necessarily mean that he or she is rejecting them or Judaism."

throughout America are discovering that some of their most committed members are "Jews-by-choice" brought to our people's Covenant with God through intermarriage. Every rabbi knows devout Jews whose spouses are not Jewish. There are even occasional non-Jewish spouses of Jews who display considerable knowledge and observance of Jewish tradition. Intermarriage among American Jewry is a complicated puzzle.

If our reaction to intermarriage has grown less hysterical over the years, it is because we have learned that intermarriage is somehow different in America than it has been in the Jewish past. In other lands, an intermarried Jew almost invariably left Judaism, while the children of intermarriages almost always identified as non-Jews. In the Soviet Union, for example, 92% of the children of Jewish intermarriages register their identity in concert with that of their non-Jewish parent when

they become eligible to make the choice at age eighteen.

In sharp contrast, American Jewish intermarriages identify predominantly with the Jewish community. The aforementioned National Jewish Population Study found that three fourths of the children of intermarried Jews were being reared as Jews. Rearing children as Jews can of course mean many different things. It may or may not entail their enrollment in a religious school. It may involve the parents in Jewish home observance, or it may consist of little more than informing their children that they are Jewish. Regardless of the definition of Jewish rearing, it does not appear that intermarriage will diminish the number of Americans who consider themselves Jewish. A few scholars have even suggested that intermarriage will produce a net increase in the Jewish population, at least in the short term. If the National Jewish Population Study statistics remain valid, intermarriage will not pose a serious threat to the future of American Jewry—numerically.

But if it will not reduce our numbers, as previously feared, why is intermarriage still considered such a threat to our Jewish future? Why do many Jewish parents get so upset when their children date non-Jews? Why do most rabbis—myself included—still decline to officiate at mixed marriages?

Intermarriage threatens the future of American Jewry—qualitatively. Our evidence is not as strong as we might like, but that danger is coming into focus. The various studies that examine the consequences of intermarriage invariably conclude that it tends to diminish many important aspects of Jewish involvement and observance. Although some intermarriages produce Jews of substantial commitment, most result in very low levels of Jewish knowledge and practice. Intermarrieds and their children attend temple services much less often and perform fewer traditional rituals at home than non-intermarrieds. They display appreciably lower levels of concern for Israel and Russian Jewry and appear to have less of a sense of Jewish Peoplehood, one of the most crucial components of Jewish identity. When their children marry, they almost invariably marry non-Jews. In short, among most intermarried families and their children who identify as Jews, their Jewishness appears so minimal, so watered-down, that some might question whether it has any meaning at all.

The intermarried families stand in stark contrast to conversionary marriages and their children, who seem to observe more faithfully and study more diligently even than those families in which both parents are born Jewish. All evidence indicates that conversion succeeds in fostering a committed Jewish identity.

Overwhelmingly, intermarrieds who join synagogues affiliate with the Reform movement. Within the next couple of decades, a sizable proportion of Reform Jewish membership will be intermarried. Some temples may find, in fact, that a majority of their members are intermarried. Even if the Outreach program never reaches outside temple walls, sufficient work will remain within the Reform movement. The impact of such an intermarried presence on temple programs will be substantial. Our future as a movement within the Jewish People may depend upon our ability to assimilate such a large percentage of intermarried families.

To what extent will we bring them into the Jewish People and make them and their offspring authentic Jews? To what extent will they diminish our distinctive Jewishness or alter its essential meaning?

Intermarriage is the linchpin in the unfolding personality of American Jewry. It occurs precisely because we Jews have attained such acceptance in America. We love our integration into the society, but we also want to preserve and enhance our unique heritage and Covenant with God. Spiraling intermarriage, even if all intermarried couples rear their children as Jews, threatens to dilute the uniqueness of Jewish identity to such an extent that Jewishness would lose its compelling character.

Many questions remain unanswered about Jewish intermarriage. Why do some Jews with strong Jewish educations marry non-Jews while others do not? Why do some non-Jewish spouses convert to Judaism while others do not? Do the children of conversionary marriages become affirmative Jewish adults? How do the children of intermarriages "reared as Jews" identify as adults? What are the most effective strategies for coping with the realities of intermarriage?

In his Biennial sermon, Rabbi Schindler proposed an extensive investigation to explore precisely such questions. The delegates later endorsed a resolution calling for this study. Our future as Reform Jews and the future of American Jewry may well depend upon the answers.　　　　✱

RELIGION AS A LANGUAGE

by Nancy Kelly Kleiman

My husband and I have been in a Mixed Marriage for ten years into which I've brought my Christian upbringing and several years training as a Roman Catholic nun, and he, a lifetime of religious training in Judaism including being both president of his Youth Group and a teacher in the Religious School, as well as, prior to our marriage, having the desire to become a Rabbi.

We have two sons who were taken to the Mikvah at birth and converted to Traditional Judaism making them the fourth generation of our family to be members of our Reform Congregation.

We chose Judaism as our family's religious expression before we married and five years before having children because it was important for us to have a common source of spiritual nourishment and, to do so, it was easier for me to reach into my Judeo-Christian heritage to find this commonality.

Because religious ties and commitment are important to both of us, I like to make an analogy of what religion means to me based on a meditation found in The Gates of Prayer:

I can no more be religious without belonging to a particular religion anymore than I can talk without using a particular language.

Consider for a moment the concept of religion as a language. Each of us was born of parents who spoke a particular language and passed this on as an accident of birth. So, too, many of us learned a religious language used to communicate about God and matters of the spirit.

I like this analogy because there is no judgment in the concept of language as a tool for communication. Those who have acquired several languages can, without diminishing the richness of their Mother tongue, read the same book in several languages with understanding, and likewise, converse with those who do not share their native speech.

Also, there is a development in language just as in one's religious beliefs. For example, a preschooler has more limitations in language mastery than a college graduate, yet they speak the same language. So, too, do we grow in religious development through education and experience.

It is in this framework that I retain my Catholic identity in the sense that I am fluent in the religious language of Catholism because that is the vehicle my parents had to teach me about God and matters of the spirit. To relinquish this identity would be to deny an integral part of who I am. As I have grown, I have been exposed to many dialects of Christianity and non-Christian beliefs all of which challenge me to remain open and accepting of differences without losing the uniqueness of my own identity.

Our children also have unique identities - they have a Jewish fahter, grandparents and family with their history, as well as a Christian mother, grandparents and family with their history. They will become fluent in the religious language of Judaism and the heritage of its People because that is the vehicle we chose to communicate with them about God and matters of the spirit. As they grow, they will be exposed to many other dialects of religion and it is our hope that they will accept the challenge to remain open and tolerant of differences without losing the uniqueness of their identities.

Christian Father, Jewish Son

*by Peter Gardella, PhD, Chairman, Religion Department,
Manhattanville College, Purchase, NY*

A week after William was born, the rabbi came to our apartment to circumcise him. My wife Lorrie and I decided to have a *Bris*,* a religious circumcision, partly because we are an intermarried couple. Otherwise, there would have been no sign of our intention to raise William as a Jew.

Not that we were ready for a *Bris*. I have no *yarmulkes* in the house, but I dug into my closet and found knit sailor hats for Lorrie's father and myself, and a wool ski hat with a brim for her brother. Since it was August, the hats contrasted nicely with our clothes. We looked more like dockworkers than worshippers.

The rabbi washed up, laid out his instruments, and said a few prayers. Then Lorrie's father, as the eldest male, had to hold the baby's legs apart while the rabbi cut the foreskin off and the rest of us watched. William cried as loudly as he could and caught his breath, again and again, to cry more loudly. Lorrie had to leave the room, then had to come back. A knot formed in my stomach that did not loosen for the rest of the day. But the rabbi soaked a gauze pad in kosher wine and gave it to William, who sucked it dry, then took another and went to sleep.

Archaic though the custom might seem (especially when medical fashion has turned against circumcision), it took the place of baptism well enough to satisfy me. With prayer but without superstition, the rabbi left a mark on William and a certificate to explain its meaning. William had earned his initiation. During the year since that day, it has become clear that I was initiated into something as well. Lorrie and I once witnessed each other's faith and shared our family holidays without practicing any rituals of our own. Now we say a blessing over every meal we have together. On Friday nights, I bring home a pizza; but before we eat it, I lift William up to watch Lorrie light two candles. We sing the blessing for the Sabbath, and then we sing a bouncy Sabbath song and dance William around. The candles burn for hours afterward, defining my favorite time of the week.

The most personal ritual happens at night. My first memory of religion is my mother standing next to my bed, saying a "Hail, Mary" and looking beatific. When I have left or considered leaving the Catholic church, the Virgin has drawn me back, and I wondered whether William would have an equal heritage. Then I noticed that when Lorrie put William into his crib, she touched his head and sang a prayer that began, "*Shema yisrael, Adonai elohenu, Adonai ehod...*" ("Hear, O Israel, the Lord is God, the Lord is One..."). When Lorrie stayed at her grandfather's house as a child, he taught this prayer to her; now she sang it to his namesake. I learned the prayer too, for the nights when I put William to bed.

Perhaps William will be glad to go to college and get away from all this piety. He won't be able to escape the heritage of Jewish-Christian conflict. One reason for raising William Jewish is that I can take part in Jewish worship without affirming anything I can't affirm; but the larger culture puts terrific pressure on Jews to accept things outside their tradition.

*Generally, the circumcision ceremony is called a *Bris*. The modern Hebrew term, however, is *Berit Milah*, meaning the covenant of circumcision.

Only one Christmas has passed since William's birth, and he loved the lights on the tree at my parents' house, but the holiday revealed the need for more decisions. I'll have to supply the tree for myself someday, and I think that I will do that, even if the tree stands in my study. Some of the Christian pressure on William will come from his father.

That pressure testifies to the paternal and filial need that Jews and Christians have of each other. Without Jews, Christians are orphans. Christians ignorant of Judaism worship a hero isolated from history, a savior of individuals with no relation to the world. Fathering a Jew makes me part of a mission that stretches from Abraham, four thousand years ago, to the kingdom of the Messiah (which Christians call the Second Coming). The connection completes my own identity, and makes it easier for me to remind other Christians of theirs.

Without Christians, Jews would lack progeny. Abraham's vision of a people as numerous as the stars in heaven or the dust of the earth looks more plausible when it includes a billion Christians alongside the world's fourteen million Jews. And it may be that William, who reverses history as a Jew with a Christian father, will contribute to another sacred paradox, the modern Judaism that understands and accepts other faiths without losing its own. He may continue the cosmopolitan faith of my father, whose Italian surname he bears.

While dreaming these dreams, I had my car serviced at a dealership in a Connecticut town. In the waiting room, I sat next to a man who casually cursed the "damn Jews. They took their money from America and sent it to Israel. Their rejection of Jesus showed that they didn't believe in God." When I asked whether any Jew had ever hurt him, he said that Felix Rohatyn had invented the New York non-resident income tax to take his money.

I called the man a bigot and a fascist, in between correcting his knowledge of history and determining that he was actually pursuing Bible studies in his church. He reminded me of the anti-Semitism of my hometown, my family, and the whole Christian world. No pope has ever sent an ambassador to Israel. Before settling down to look for the Messiah I should remember to pray that my brothers and sisters in Christ tolerate my son.

Newsreach, Vol. 4, No. 1
January – March 1987.

PARTICIPANT'S EVALUATION OF "TIMES AND SEASONS: A JEWISH PERSPECTIVE"

1. What was most helpful for you?

2. What was least helpful to you?

3. What recommendations would you make for future groups?

4. Is there anything else you want us to know?

5. Would you like to be contacted by a synagogue near you?

"THE TIMES AND THE SEASONS: A JEWISH PERSPECTIVE FOR INTERMARRIED COUPLES"

DATE: _____

OVERALL, PLEASE RATE THIS WORKSHOP IN TERMS

	(1) Excellent	(2) Very Good	(3) Good	(4) Fair	(5) Poor
1. Relevance of Material Presented					
2. Organization of Course					
3. Maintenance of Interest and Involvement					
4. Your Own Participation					
5. Room Setting/Comfort					
TO WHAT EXTENT WAS THE PRESENTER					
6. Knowledgeable about the subject matter presented					
7. Able to hold your interest in the material being presented					
8. Organized and effective in the delivery of the course					
9. Able to incorporate handout material which enhance the course					
10. Able to involve the participants in the course					
11. HOW WOULD YOU RATE THIS PROGRAM OVERALL?					

12. Would you recommend this program to a friend?   (1) yes _____   (2) no _____

Comments: _____

13. Will the information presented have an impact on your life   (1) yes _____   (2) no _____

14. What did you think was the most helpful part of the program? _____

_____

The least helpful? _____   _____

15. How could the program's effectiveness be improved? _____

_____

16. Are there any courses/workshops which you would like to see presented in the future? _____

17. Is there anything else you'd like us to know? _____

Sex:

(1) Female
(2) Male

Approximate Age:

(1) 16-20
(2) 21-25
(3) 26-35

(4) 36-45
(5) 46-55
(6) 56-65

Religious Background _____

18. Would you like to be contacted by a synagogue near you?   (1)yes _____   (2)no _____

THANK YOU FOR YOUR COOPERATION

REPORT OF THE COMMITTEE ON PATRILINEAL DESCENT
ON THE STATUS OF CHILDREN OF MIXED MARRIAGES

The purpose of this document is to establish the Jewish status of the children of mixed marriages in the Reform Jewish community of North America.

One of the most pressing human issues for the North American Jewish community is mixed marriage, with all its attendant implications. For our purpose mixed marriage is defined as a union between a Jew and a non-Jew. A non-Jew who joins the Jewish people through conversion is recognized as a Jew in every respect. We deal here only with the Jewish identity of children born of a union in which one parent is Jewish and the other parent is non-Jewish.

According to the Halachah as interpreted by traditional Jews over many centuries, the offspring of a Jewish mother and a non-Jewish father is recognized as a Jew, while the offspring of a non-Jewish mother and a Jewish father is considered a non-Jew. To become a Jew the child of a non-Jewish mother and a Jewish father must undergo conversion.

As a Reform community, the process of determining an appropriate response has taken us to an examination of the tradition, our own earlier responses and the most current considerations. In doing so, we seek to be sensitive to the human dimension of this issue.

Both the Biblical and the rabbinical traditions take for granted that ordinarily the paternal line is decisive in the tracing of descent within the Jewish people. The Biblical genealogies in Genesis and elsewhere in the Bible attest to this point. In intertribal marriage in ancient Israel, paternal descent was decisive. Numbers 1:2, etc., says: "By their families, by their fathers' houses" (le-mishpehotam le-veit avotam), which for the rabbis means "The line (literally: 'family') of the father is recognized; the line of the mother is not" (mishpahat av keruyah mishpahah; mishpahat eim einah keruyah mishpahah; Baba Batra 109b, Yebamot 54b; cf. Yad, Nahalot 1:6).

In the rabbinic tradition, this tradition remains in force. The offspring of a male kohen who marries a Levite or Israelite is considered a kohen and the child of an Israelite who marries a kohenet is an Israelite. Thus yichus, lineage, regards the male line as absolutely dominant. This ruling is stated succinctly in Mishnah Kiddushin 3:12 that when kiddushin (marriage) is licit and no transgression (ein avera) is involved the line follows the father. Furthermore, the most important parental responsibility to teach Torah rested with the father (Kiddushin 29a; cf. Shulchan Aruch Yore De-ah 245:1).

When, in the tradition, the marriage was considered not to be licit, the child of that marriage followed the status of the mother (Mishnah Kiddushin 3:12, ha-velad Kemotah). The decisions of our ancestors thus to link the child inseparably to the mother, which makes the child of a Jewish mother Jewish and the child of a non-Jewish mother non-Jewish, regardless of the father, was based upon the fact that the woman with her child had no recourse but to return to her own people. A Jewish woman could not marry a non-Jewish man (cf. Shulchan Aruch, Even Ha-ezer 4:19, la tafsei kiddushin). A Jewish man could not marry a non-Jewish woman. The only recourse in rabbinic law for the woman in either case was to return to her own community and people.

Since Emancipation, Jews have faced the problem of mixed marriage and the status of the offspring of mixed marriage. The Reform Movement responded to the issue. In 1947 The CCAR adopted a proposal made by the Committee on Mixed Marriage and Intermarriage:

> With regard to infants, the declaration of the parents to raise them as Jews shall be deemed sufficient for conversion. This could apply, for example, to adopted children. This decision is in line with the traditional procedure in which, according to the Talmud, the parents bring young children (the Talmud speaks of children earlier than the age of three) to be converted, and the Talmud comments that although an infant cannot give its consent, it is permissable to benefit somebody without his consent (or presence). On the same page the Talmud also speaks of a father bringing his children for conversion, and says that the children will be satisfied with the action of their father. If the parents therefore will make a declaration to the rabbi that it is their intention to raise the child as a Jew, the child may, for the sake of impressive formality, be recorded in the Cradle-Roll of the religious school and thus be considered converted.

Children of religious school age should likewise not be required to undergo a special ceremony of conversion but should receive instruction as regular students in the school. The ceremony of Confirmation at the end of the school course shall be considered in lieu of a conversion ceremony.

Children older than confirmation age should not be converted without their own consent. The Talmudic law likewise gives the child who is converted in infancy by the court the right to reject the conversion when it becomes of religious age. Therefore the child above religious school age, if he or she consents sincerely to conversion, should receive regular instruction for that purpose and be converted in the regular conversion ceremony." (Vol. 57, CCAR Annual)

This issue was again addressed in the 1961 edition of the Rabbi's Manual:

Jewish law recognizes a person as Jewish if his mother was Jewish, even though the father was not a Jew. One born of such mixed parentage may be admitted to membership in the synagogue and enter into a marital relationship with a Jew, provided he has not been reared in or formally admitted into some other faith. The child of a Jewish father and a non-Jewish mother, according to traditional law, is a Gentile; such a person would have to be formally converted in order to marry a Jew or become a synagogue member.

Reform Judaism, however, accepts such a child as Jewish without a formal conversion, if he attends a Jewish school and follows a course of studies leading to Confirmation. Such procedure is regarded as sufficient evidence that the parents and the child himself intend that he shall live as a Jew. (p. 112, Rabbi's Manual.)

We face today an unprecedented situation due to the changed conditions in which decisions concerning the status of the child of a mixed marriage are to be made. There are tens of thousands of mixed marriages. In a vast majority of these cases the non-Jewish extended family is a functioning part of the child's world, and may be decisive in shaping the life of the child. It can no longer be assumed a priori, therefore, that the child of a Jewish mother will be Jewish any more than that the child of a non-Jewish mother will not be.

This leads us to the conclusion that the same requirements must be applied to establish the status of a child of a mixed marriage, regardless of whether the mother or the father is Jewish.

Therefore:

The Jewish status of the offspring of any mixed marriage is established

through appropriate and timely public and formal acts of identification
with the Jewish faith and people. The performance of these mitzvot serves
to commit those who participate in them, both parent and child, to Jewish
life.

Depending on circumstances,[1] mitzvot leading toward a positive and
exclusive Jewish identity will include entry into the covenant, acquisition
of a Hebrew name, Torah study, bar/bat mitzvah and Kabbalat Torah
(Confirmation).[2] For those beyond childhood claiming Jewish identity,
other public acts or declarations may be added or substituted after
consultation with their rabbi.

---

1. According to the age or setting, parents should consult a rabbi to determine the
specific mitzvot which are necessary.

2. A full description of these and other mitzvot can be found in Shaarei Mitzvah.

QUESTIONS AND ANSWERS ON JEWISH DESCENT

Clarifying the Jewish Identity of the Child of a Mixed Marriage

Since the adoption by the Central Conference of American Rabbis of the Report of the Committee on the Status of Children of Mixed Marriages (Patrilineal Descent) in March, 1983, the committee has continued to examine the implications of the new position in the light of particular situations. The following format of question and response is presented to clarify the position, its background and intent, and its application to individual circumstances. The committee welcomes additional queries and reports, which should be addressed to the Central Conference of American Rabbis, 21 E. 40 St., New York, NY 10016.

QUESTION 1 - Is the CCAR Resolution a Form of Legislation?

The resolution is, in its own words, a declaration. The CCAR has never seen itself as a body that legislates halachically. It interprets, it advises, it issues responsa, it declares - by majority vote - the opinion of its membership arrived at in an open convention or through a mail poll.

QUESTION 2 - Is It the Intent of the Resolution to make the Establishment of Jewish Identity in the Case of a Mixed Marriage Dependent on More Than Descent From a Jewish Parent?

Yes, identity is seen as derivable from a Jewish parent, but finally determined in the life of the individual through public acts and the pattern of living.

QUESTION 3 - Does the Resolution Consider the Establishment of the Jewish Identity of Children of Mixed Marriages to be Established in Exactly the Same Manner No Matter Which Parent Is Jewish?

Yes.

QUESTION 4 - Are the _Mitzvot_ Mentioned in the Resolution as Ways
of Establishing the Jewish Identity of the Children of Mixed
Marriages Mandatory?

The list given is intended to be descriptive and is neither
mandatory nor complete. Not listed, but obviously relevant, would
be such _mitzvot_ as regular attendance at worship or a pattern of
participation in Jewish causes.

QUESTION 5 - What is meant by the _Mitzvah_ of Torah Study?

Learning which assumes both commitment and knowledge as
carried out under rabbinic supervision, preferably in a synagogue
setting.

QUESTION 6 - Are There Traditional Precedents for the 1983
Resolution?

The historic grounds for the conclusion of this resolution
which departs from longstanding halachic decision were discussed
in a recent responsum which may be obtained from the CCAR.

Recruiting for "Times and Seasons..." and Sample
Publicity and Registration Materials

Recruiting for this program can be difficult and frustrating.
Our primary target population is intermarried and intermarrying
couples unaffiliated with the Jewish community. While we know
that there are hundreds of thousands of them in North America,
they can often be difficult to find. It is important to remember
that while recruiting may be extremely difficult in the beginning,
it will get easier. Many graduates of "Times and Seasons..." tell
their friends about the program.

All rabbis, educators and administrators should have information about the program on hand, (and should be reminded each
time a new group is scheduled) since they often come in contact
with potential participants.

News releases should be sent to temple bulletins (remember
to send them well in advance of publication deadlines), and
Jewish newspapers. Even though the participants may be unaffiliated and may not see these papers themselves, they may have
friends and relatives who do and who may send them the information.

News releases should also be sent to major newspapers and
neighborhood newspapers. They may decide to include the information. Alternatively, once the program has occurred, it might
be possible to interest a reporter in doing a story on the
issue of intermarriage and how couples deal with them. Such a
story, responsibly reported, gains the program visibility and
will probably make future recruiting somewhat easier.

Flyers about the program can be place in the rear of the
temple with other informational material. Often unaffiliated
intermarried couples come to temple for weddings, b'nai mitzvah,
funerals or other occasions.

Do not underestimate the value of "word-of-mouth" advertising.
Spread word of this program everywhere you go, to everyone with
whom you come in contact. Ask for names.

It is important to develop a list of names from all these
sources. This list then can be augmented, updated, etc. as
circumstances warrant. Each time a group is scheduled, a mailing
announcing date, time, etc. should go out to everyone on the list.
We have known instances when a couple was on our list for three
years and finally enrolled in "Times and Seasons...". Ideally,
the mailing should be followed up by a telephone call. Often
one or both partners may be hesitant to respond to the mailing.
A personal phone call, however, can be very effective. A warm,
friendly voice can communicate a great deal, both spoken and
unspoken to one who may be hesitant to begin the group.

Nursery schools are often good places to recruit. Many
nursery schools have high persentages of intermarried couples.

Commission on Reform Jewish Outreach

UNION OF AMERICAN HEBREW CONGREGATIONS — CENTRAL CONFERENCE OF AMERICAN RABBIS

6300 WILSHIRE BOULEVARD, SUITE 1475, LOS ANGELES, CALIFORNIA 90048 (213) 653-9962

איחוד
ליהדות
מתקדמת
באמריקה

December, 1985

Every couple must deal with many issues as they build their life together. In a marriage between a Jew and one who is of another faith, such concerns as separating from family, establishing a home, working out a balance between the need for closeness and the need for individuation are often complicated by real differnces in background and experience. Strong feelings arise for both members of the couple as well as their extended families. Often the couple must deal with these issues without much support or background information from the family and the community.

We would like to invite you to participate in "The Times and The Seasons: A Jewish Perspective for Interfaith Couples," an innovative program which will serve as a framework for open and frank discussions about concerns and issues in interfaith marriage. You will come together with other interfaith couples in a comfortable non-judgmental environment and share your personal concerns about children, families, expectations (stated and unstated) with each other and with your fellow group members. During the course of our eight (8) sessions together you will also have the opportunity to clarify questions which you might have about Jewish traditions, beliefs and practices. It is our hope that this dialogue and expanded understanding will deepen the relationship between partners in an interfaith couple.

This program is offered by the Union of American Hebrew Congregations as part of its National Outreach Program, with the generous support of the Louis Wolfson Institute and the National Federation of Temple Sisterhoods. Those couples who have participated in it have found it to be extremely helpful. We hope you will join us in this exciting program. The cost is $50.00 per couple for eight (8) weeks. We plan to offer this program at:

        University Synagogue
        11960 Sunset Blvd.
        Los Angeles, CA 90049
        Thursday, January 9 - February 20, 1986

Please fill out the enclosed registration form and return it to us with your check for $50.00 made payable to the UAHC.

If you have any questions or want to discuss the program further, please call Mickey Finn at (213)653-9962.

                    Sincerely,

Chairman
David W. Belin
Co-Chairmen
Rabbi Steven Foster
Director
Lydia Kukoff
    Los Angeles

Lydia Kukoff
Director

-172-

Rabbi Joel Oseran
Facilitator

THE TIMES AND THE SEASONS: A JEWISH PERSPECTIVE FOR INTERFAITH COUPLES

Registration Form

Union of American Hebrew Congregations
6300 Wilshire Blvd., Suite 1475   Los Angeles, CA. 90048
(213) 653-9962

Santa Monica Session
Santa Monica Synagogue
958 Linclon Blvd.
Santa Monica, CA 90403
Tuesday, January 13 to
February 24, 1987
7:30 - 9:30 PM
Rabbi Jeffrey Perry-Marx,
Facilitator

Valley Session
Temple Judea
5429 Lindley Ave.
Tarzana, CA 91356
Thursday, January 22
to March 5, 1987
7:30 - 9:30 PM
Rabbi John Moscowitz
Facilitator

Orange County
Temple Beth David
6100 Hefley St.
Westminster, CA 92683
Wednesday, January 7
to February 18, 1987
7:30 - 9:30 PM
Ms. Judy Green,
Facilitator

****

NAME:_____NAME OF SPOUSE:_____

ADDRESS:_____CITY;_____ZIP:_____

PHONE:(home)_____(business)_____BIRTH DATE:_____

OCCUPATION:_____

YEARS MARRIED:_____AGE & SEX OF CHILDREN:_____

RELIGION:_____RELIGIOUS TRAINING:_____

_____

HAVE YOU TAKEN THE UAHC INTRODUCTION TO JUDAISM COURSE?_____

LOCATION PREFERENCE: SANTA MONICA_____VALLEY_____ORANGE COUNTY_____

WHAT SPECIAL NEEDS DO YOU HAVE?_____

_____

_____

WHAT ARE YOUR EXPECTATIONS OF THIS PROGRAM?_____

_____

_____

_____

_____

_____

_____

DATE OF REGISTRATION:_____

TO EVERY THING THERE IS A SEASON. AND A TIME TO EVERY PURPOSE UNDER THE HEAVEN.....

"THE TIMES & THE SEASONS: A JEWISH PERSPECTIVE for INTERFAITH COUPLES"

Every couple must deal with many issues as they build their life together. In a marriage between a Jew and one who is of another faith, such concerns as separating from family, establishing a home, working out a balance between the need for closeness and the need for individuation are often complicated by real differences in background and experience. Strong feelings arise for both members of the couple as well as their extended families. Often the couple must deal with these issues without much support or background information from the family and the community.

We would like to invite you to participate in "THE TIMES AND THE SEASONS: A JEWISH PERSPECTIVE FOR INTERFAITH COUPLES," an innovative program which will serve as a framework for open and frank discussions about concerns and issues in interfaith marriage. You will come together with other interfaith couples in a comfortable non-judgemental environment and share your personal concerns about children, families, expectations (stated and unstated) with each other and with your fellow group members. During the course of our eight (8) sessions together you will also have the opportunity to clarify questions which you might have about Jewish traditions, beliefs and practices. It is our hope that this dialogue and expanded understanding will deepen the relationship between partners in an interfaith couple.

8 CONSECUTIVE

Wednesday evenings
7:30 - 9:30 p.m.

CLASSES BEGIN

Wednesday, April 17, 1985

at CONGREGATION

Temple Shaaray Tefila
Baldwin Hill Road
Bedford, New York 10506

For further information please
call Dru Greenwood (201) 599-0080

SPONSORED BY: UAHC-CCAR COMMISSION ON REFORM JEWISH OUTREACH

איחור
להבות
סתכרמת

TIMES and SEASONS: A Liberal Jewish Perspective on Intermarriage

You are invited to participate in an innovative program of open and frank discussion about concerns and issues in interfaith marriage.

You will come together with other interfaith couples in a supportive, comfortable and non-judgmental setting to share your personal ideas about family holidays, raising children and other interfaith issues.

This program is not conversionary, coercive or manipulative in any way. However, it is a Jewish program, offered in a Jewish setting, by an experienced facilitator. During the course of our eight sessions together you will have the opportunity to clarify questions you might have about Jewish tradition, belief and practices.

This program has been developed under the auspices of the Commission on Reform Jewish Outreach and is sponsored by the Northeast Council of the Union of American Hebrew Congregations under the direction of Nancy Kelly Kleiman, Regional Outreach Coordinator.

Our group facilitator is Deborah Whitehill, L.I.C.S.W., who has had extensive experience facilitating such groups in the greater Boston area. We are delighted she will be leading our program!

Registration for Times and Seasons is limited to eight couples. Cost of the eight-week program is $75.00 per couple. The Fall session will be held:

    TIME: *Thursday evenings from 7:30PM to 9:30PM beginning October 9, 1986*

    PLACE: *Union of American Hebrew Congregations 1330 Beacon Street, Suite 355 Brookline, MA 02146*

For further information please contact Nancy Kelly Kleiman at the above address or by calling 617,277-1655.

SOME QUESTIONS RAISED IN THE DISCUSSION SERIES:

    How do we raise our children?
    What faith should our children practice?
    My in-laws don't feel comfortable that I'm not Jewish - How do I deal with this?
    I know I don't want to convert to Judaism - Can my home still be Jewish? Will I be welcome at a synagogue service?

Times and Seasons

Every couple must deal with many issues as they build their life together. In a marriage between a Jew and one who is of another faith, such concerns as separating from family, establishing a home, working out a balance between the need for closeness and the need for individuation are often complicated by real differences in background and experience. Strong feelings arise for both members of the couple as well as their extended families. Often the couple must deal with these issues without much support or background information from the family and the community.

We would like to invite you to participate in "THE TIMES AND THE SEASONS: A JEWISH PERSPECTIVE FOR INTERFAITH COUPLES," an innovative program which will serve as a framework for open and frank discussions about concerns and issues in interfaith marriage. You will come together with other interfaith couples in a comfortable non-judgemental environment and share your personal concerns about children, families, expectations (stated and unstated) with each other and with your fellow group members. During the course of our eight (8) sessions together you will also have the opportunity to clarify questions which you might have about Jewish traditions, beliefs and practices.

THREE SESSIONS

DATE AND PLACE:

Santa Monica Synagogue
Tuesday, January 12, 1987
thru February 12, 1987
Rabbi Jeffrey Perry-Marx
Facilitator

Temple Judea
Thursday, January 22, 1987
thru March 5, 1987
Rabbi John Moscowitz,
Facilitator

Temple Beth David
Wednesday, January 7, 1987
thru February 18, 1987
Ms. Judy Green, Facilitator

TIME:

7:30 - 9:30 PM

FEE:

$75.00 per couple
Make checks payable to
the UAHC

PRE-REGISTRATION IS REQUIRED

For further information call
Arlene Chernow or Mickey Finn
at (213) 653-9962

******

Sample release for temple bulletins or newspapers

<u>F O R   I M M E D I A T E   R E L E A S E</u>

<u>TIMES AND SEASONS: A JEWISH PERSPECTIVE FOR INTERMARRIED COUPLES</u>

The Pacific Southwest Council of the UAHC is sponsoring a pilot
program for unaffiliated intermarried couples (and couples
contemplating intermarriage). The goal of the program is to
make the couples more comfortable with Judaism by focusing
on issues raised by Jewish holiday and life cycle obsevances
in a supportive environment. Theprogram, beginning in
October, will run for eight weeks. The cost is $50.00 per
couple.

If you would like more information about this innovative
program, or if you know anyone who might be interested in
participating, please call the UAHC office, (213)653-9962
and ask for Lydia Kukoff or Mickey Finn.

OUTREACH PROGRAM BANK
Scenarios and Strategies

TITLE: "Mary and Herb"

AIM: To broaden participants' understanding of the difficulty of problems that may be encountered in an intermarriage and to provide tools for considering solutions.

NOTE: This exercise can be done by individuals, couples or small groups. It is important to insure that all categories are included. If the exercise is done in small groups, the groups then return to the larger group to report. The facilitator should not answer any questions regarding specifics of the scenario not included and should state that the exercise is deliberately ambiguous. Participants may be frustrated if unable to come up with a "solution" and will sometimes state that this is an extreme case. It may be helpful to respond that it is dramatic, but that the feelings and dilemma are common.

* * * * * * * * * * * * * * * *

Mary and Herb Kushner have just had their first child, a boy. They had never discussed birth rituals previously, feeling that they would make the necessary decisions when the time came. Now that their son is born, they are aware of very strong feelings on the part of both sets of parents. Herb's parents are concentration camp survivors who lost their entire families in the holocaust. They are very excited about the bris that they are sure will be held for their new grandson. Mary's father, Edward O'Brian, is dying of cancer. He has been a good Catholic all his life, and he has expressed a strong desire to have his grandson baptized.

Please discuss the situation with your group, considering the following:

1. What are the <u>feelings</u> of each person above? (When in doubt, imagine!)

2. What should Mary and Herb do? List three possible solutions or approaches.

3. List three <u>funny</u> solutions. (Be outrageous!)

4. Select the best solution from the above and be prepared to discuss your choice and reasoning with the group.

Sherri Alper, A.C.S.W.

Guidelines for Cost

    The cost for the program is usually between $75.00 - $100.00 per couple. This includes the eight group sessions plus all materials. The facilitator is usually paid $50.00 per session.
    This fee structure allows the group to be self sustaining. Subsidies for couples who need financial assistance should be made available.

SELECTED BIBLIOGRAPHY

Note to facilitators: The following suggested resources are only a sampling of the various publications that are available. We have selected materials which are easily accessible and provide the basic background information needed for the discussions that may take place in your "Times and Seasons" group.

BASIC JUDAISM

Bial, Morrison D. Liberal Judaism at Home: The Practices of Modern Reform Judaism. Revised edition. Union of American Hebrew Congregations, 1971.

Maslin, Simeon J., ed. Gates of Mitzvah. Central Conference of American Rabbis, 1979.

Steinberg, Milton. Basic Judaism. Harcourt Brace Jovanovich, 1947.

Syme, Daniel B. The Jewish Home Series. Union of American Hebrew Congregations.

CHRISTIANITY AND JUDAISM

Goldberg, Michael. Jews and Christians: Getting Our Stories Straight. Abingdon Press, Nashville 1985.

Sandmel, Samuel. We Jews and Jesus. Oxford University Press, 1973.

Weiss-Rosmarin, Trude. Judaism and Christianity: The Differences. Jonathan David, 1965.

HISTORY

Bamberger, Bernard J. The Story of Judaism. Schocken 1964.

Margolis, Max L. and Marx, Alexander. A History of the Jewish People. Atheneum, 1977.

Roth Cecil. A History of the Jews: From the Earliest Times Through the Six Day War. Revised edition. Schocken 1970.

Sachar, Howard M. The Course of Modern Jewish History. Dell, 1977.

Seltzer, Robert M. Jewish People, Jewish Thought: The Jewish Experience in History. Macmillan, 1980.

HOLIDAYS, FESTIVALS AND THE SABBATH

A Shabbat Manual. Central Conference of American Rabbis, 1983.

Stern, Chaim, ed. Gates of the Seasons. Central Conference of American Rabbis, 1983.

Syme, Daniel B. The Jewish Home Series. Union of American Hebrew Congregations.

HOLOCAUST

Altshuler, David A. A young reader's version of Hitler's War Against the Jews: 1935-1945 by Lucy S. Dawidowicz. Behrman House.

ISRAEL

Hertzberg, Arthur, ed. The Zionist Idea. Atheneum, 1959.

Sachar, Howard M. A History of Israel: From the Rise of Zionism to Our Time. Knopf, 1979.

THEOLOGY

Borowitz, Eugene. Modern Varieties of Jewish Thought: A Presentation and Interpretation. Behrman House, 1981.

Borowitz, Eugene. Understanding Judaism. Union of American Hebrew Congregations, 1979.

Borowitz, Eugene. Choices in Modern Jewish Thought: A Partisan Guide. Behrman House, 1983.

Syme, Daniel and Sonsino, Rifat. Finding God. Union of American Hebrew Congregaions, 1986.

CONVERSION AND INTERMARRIAGE

Belin, David. Why Choose Judaism: New Dimensions of Jewish Outreach. Union of American Hebrew Congregations, 1985.

Compass: New Directions in Jewish Education. "Interfaith Marriages." Union of American Hebrew Congregations, 1984.

Friedman, Edwin H. "The Myth of the Shiksa." Ethnicity and Family Therapy. Guilford Press, NY 1982.

Guidelines for Outreach Education. Union of American Hebrew Congregations, Fall 1986.

Mayer, Egon. Love and Tradition: Marriage Between Jews and Christians. Plenum Press, NY 1985.

Mayer, Egon and Avgar, Amy. <u>Conversion Among the Intermarried:</u>
<u>Choosing to Become Jewish</u>. American Jewish Committee 1987.

Sandmel, Samuel. <u>When a Jew and Christian Marry</u>. Fortress Press,
Philadelphia 1977.

<u>GENERAL REFERENCES</u> - Jewish:

<u>Encyclopedia Judaica</u> (selected subject headings)

Jacobs, L. <u>The Book of Jewish Belief</u>. Behrman House.

<u>Keeping Posted</u>

<u>America</u>:
" 1873, 1973, 2073: A Glimpse into the Jewish Community"
"A Century of German Jewish Immigration"
"The Golden Land (Eastern European Immigration)"

<u>Concepts</u>:
"Tzedakah"
"Jewish Symbols"
"Who Is A Jew?"

<u>Ethics, Law, and Issues</u>:
"Jewish Law"
"A Time to be Born...A Time to Die"
"Why Do the Innocent Suffer?"

<u>Holocaust</u>:
"Aspects of the Holocaust"
"Righteous Gentiles"

<u>Israel and Zionism</u>:
"Zionism"
"Jerusalem:Why are the Nations in an Uproar? (The importance of
Jerusalem)"
"The Covenant (The people, the land)"
"Israel-Diaspora"

<u>Jewish Movements</u>:
"The Chasid"
"What is Reform?"
"Orthodox Judaism"
"Conservative Judaism"
"Reconstructionist Judaism"
"The Sephardim"

<u>Judaism and Christianity</u>:
"The Messiah Idea, False Messiah, Modern Pied Pipers"
"Judaism and Christianity: Parting of the Ways"
"A Missionary Faith? (Shall Jews seek converts?)

Love, Marriage, Family:
"The Jewish Family: Continuity and Change"
"Love, Marriage, Intermarriage"
"Peace in the Home"

Traditional Texts and Holidays:
"The Hebrew Bible"
"About Prayer and Prayerbooks"
"The Mishnah"
"Passover Haggadah"
"Roots of Chanukah"
"Midrash (Folk tales and folklore)"
"The Sabbath"
"Understanding the Bible"
"The Harvest Festivals"

Theology and Mysticism:
"Jewish Views of God"
"Jewish Mysticism"

Klein, Isaac. A Guide to Jewish Religious Practice. Jewish Theological Seminary, 1979.

Latner, Helen. The Book of Modern Jewish Etiquette. Schocken Books, 1981.

GENERAL REFERENCES - Counseling:

Egon, Girard. Skilled Helper. Brooks Cole Publishers, Monterey 1975.

Hackney, Harold and Nye, Sherilyn. Counseling Strategies and Objectives. Prentice-Hall.

Paterson, C.N. Relationship Counseling and Psychotherapy. Harper and Row.